Seven Nights in Israel – *A Journey of Self-Discovery*

Charta Calamum

COPYRIGHT

ISBN: 978-1-7395611-3-0

For privacy reasons, some names, locations, and dates may have been changed.

Photography

@TheLakeEye

Script

@Charta.Calamum

Cover design by Raúl Lázaro.

DEDICATION

This book is dedicated to the *Land* in which I found inspiration. She is known to some as Israel, others as Palestine, and others as Canaan or the Holy Land.

May peace be upon her.

PROLOGUE

"The whole object of travel is not to set foot on foreign land; it is at last to set foot on one's own country as a foreign land."

Gilbert K. Chesterton, from *The Riddle of the Ivy*

1

Sunday – Clouds Are Calling

What is the time? I typically ask this question several times a day during the dark winter months. However, this question was the last thing on my mind as I stood on the edge of a rooftop, three storeys high, staring down a dark wall within one of the world's most volatile regions, the West Bank of Israel.

My story had its genesis a week prior while attempting to book a holiday to Morocco, taking the advice of friends and colleagues who had convincingly boasted of the food, culture, and lifestyle. After several hours of browsing, I had secured a flight, rental car, and hotel. As I glanced over my passport details before submitting the travel information, I caught sight of a partially concealed name scribbled on the notepad beneath. It was a name I had unintentionally forgotten but still held close to my heart. Our daily conversations had ceased in the last months, but she had taken up much of my focus for someone I'd never met. Amidst a burst of memories, I scanned the portal for flights to Israel, and a long list was loaded, most serviced by El Al, the trusted national Israeli airline that has operated for over 80 years.

Further down the page were some much cheaper, off-peak flights courtesy of WizzAir. My interest in Morocco was waning, and when I glanced at the name on the notepad again, the destinations appeared equally appealing. Now saddled with indecision, my gaze settled on the coin marked with red ink beneath the monitor, which, at that moment, seemed to be symbolic. I flipped the coin and watched as it landed with the tail facing up in the palm of my hand. The decision had been made: I was going to Israel.

On a cloudy Sunday in early December, I fought through a congested Gatwick Airport. In the lounge, the busy runway formed my primary source of entertainment, but the distraction was short-lived when the flight was announced.

People rushed to their feet, tightly clutching jackets, duty-free bags, books, phones, and passports. They evacuated the seating area like a wave departing the seashore, yet I was oblivious to the automated announcement or maybe ignored it, choosing instead to wait patiently. I calmly drew a slow, deep breath and sighed while my eyes slid shut, basking in the sudden declutter of space, enjoying the borrowed moment of tranquillity. Stillness had never felt so good—or maybe it did, and I had just forgotten amid all the recent personal chaos.

Two months earlier, with the launch of a new project at work, I found myself buried up to my neck in a heap of planning and testing, marking the start of a string of late nights, tied to my desk, exhausted eyes fixed to the computer screen. As overwhelming as it felt at the time, the workload was bearable, but a self-inflicted attempt to write my first book on top of those commitments was the straw that broke the camel's back. This last-minute trip couldn't have come at a better time.

As I walked through the cold and damp streets of Covent Garden, I pushed through a mob of bargain hunters. The plan was to find a Bureau de Change, but after a long search, I almost abandoned the idea. However, I finally located a portable exchange kiosk on Oxford Street, where I purchased a wallet full of Israeli shekels. Despite the triumph, my calves were now aching, pulsating from my boots pounding the pavement. Approaching Tottenham Court Road station, I caught a glimpse of a scarfed woman weaving through the crowded street. For a brief moment, my mind wandered, and Ama-gi (the name scribbled on the notepad) sparked a burning thought. I pictured her walking through the sandy streets of Israel, head covered in a shawl with a long linen tunic fluttering in the air. I felt a sudden rush, sensing that this trip would be life-changing, and the bulging wallet in my pocket was now a constant reminder.

The overhead tannoy crackled again, which brought me back to consciousness.

"Calling final passengers for flight TLV666W to Tel Aviv. The gate is now closing."

I reached for my rucksack and briskly proceeded towards the boarding area. When I arrived at the gate, passengers swamped the front section; among them, a group scattered near the desk stood out: the men wore identical tailored black suits and distinctive fur *shtreimel* hats worn by the Haredi (Orthodox) Jewish men. The outfits of the Haredi women weren't as uniform as the men's; their skirts and coats were primarily black or with a dull dark hue, though the similarities ended there. In close proximity, the delicate embroidery and partially concealed, shimmering jewellery disclosed their varying levels of affluence. Most of the women hovered near their partners; it was easy to identify the couples. Less conspicuous, buried behind the hues of casual outfits, skullcaps crowned the heads of a handful of men. I had never seen so many Haredi Jews in one place and under one roof. Sights of them alone or with family and generally moving at a brisk pace was a familiar experience of mine.

The general mood at the desk was cheerful, with the travellers shaking hands and exchanging warm greetings. This was my first peek behind the cultural wall, far from the watered-down stories taught at Sunday school in my early years or the recent Hollywood dramatisations such as the *Unorthodox* TV series. It felt novel, even private, to watch this group of people. I wrestled with my mind, feeling like an intruder, but as the boarding process began, I put those feelings aside and navigated past the boarding gate.

We were ushered to the flight apron, and the scent of combusted fuel in the crosswind gripped me with a ripple of excitement and the pull of anxiety. As we lined the tarmac, I glanced at a larger El Al airline crawling along the runway, making a visual comparison. With no notable external difference in the condition of the planes, I was thrilled with the substantial bargain I had made with my WizzAir choice. As I ascended the stairs, I saw an anxious young man leaning over the railing and gazing at something beneath the steps; his head swayed back and forth, and his sidelocks swung like a pendulum beneath his *shtreimel.* Intrigued, I peeked behind the stairs and saw an airport worker hastily tagging a stack of prams under the faint shade of the plane.

I was the last passenger to board the plane, and behind me, the female attendant called out, "Boarding complete!" before closing and clamping the door sealed. The passengers, however, expressed little desire to depart as they crawled to their seats, with more lingering along the aisle. At the rear of the plane, a shortened row housed two empty seats wedged against the rear cabin wall with the backrest inclined upward. Desiring a row to myself, I swiftly abandoned my allocated seat and lodged myself between the armrests of the window seat.

A peaceful, unexpected silence swept through the plane, leaving the passengers scanning the cabin, but chatting soon resumed, filling the length of space with noise. Restless, I attempted to rekindle myself with the experience of flying, but the thought opened the door to more anxiety, which left my mind racing. I had never enjoyed flying. But there was little time to think; it was time for take-off. At the edge of a clear runway, the plane was poised and vibrated with a low rumbling sound before it gently crept forward. I anticipated each step ahead to ease the tension, but the sudden acceleration broke the suspense; the plane jolted forward with a burst of speed, bobbing the nose cone up and down as the wings swayed and flaps yawned with the slight elevation. The plane's cockpit took to the air, with the fuselage following as the engines thrust the aircraft into the sky.

Vertigo began to set in as my eardrums popped. However, a thick curtain of mist that had just clothed the exterior of the portholes was a welcomed distraction. A sweaty stain marked my seat handle when I loosened my grip while trying to gain some control of my fears.

A queue of passengers had gathered next to my seat, each waiting their turn for the toilet. By now, I had got used to the tight space and felt grateful for my earlier restroom visit in the departure lounge.

It had been three years since my last international trip, and since then, my passion for travelling had withered, buried behind the doors of the Covid lockdowns. Now, I felt a jolt of excitement faintly marred with low expectations.

Growing up, I had heard so much about Israel from Sunday school classes, the odd church sermon, world news, tech hubs and, last but not least, relatives who had made an annual Christian pilgrimage to Jerusalem. It was a tradition I considered overzealous and one I had silently decided to avoid. However, it felt strange to be making my own pilgrimage, of sorts, but I was delighted to be travelling again and knew that by keeping low expectations, I could avoid disappointment.

The plane soared rapidly over the English Channel and then swung left over French shores. The sight in the distance, far below, brought memories of a weekend trip to Paris. I named the point over the channel "Ultimus Locus" because it was the final region of a holiday marathon, which had seen me visit Zurich, Madrid, Barcelona, Malaga, Venice, Rome,

Milan, Brussels, and many other major European cities.

The clouds retreated below the plane line, and the cabin walls became illuminated with a sudden amber glow. The passengers gathered like a moth to a flame, leaning towards the windows, hoping to catch a glimpse. The clouds unclothed the midday sky, and the sun stood naked as the day she was born. An echo of gasps stretched through the air as mobile phones knocked heads while passengers tried to capture the moment. The exhibition was brief, and the sun slid out of sight, leaving a blissfully quiet ambience behind.

I was overwhelmed by the harmony in the cabin and struggled to hold back my smile. The scene along the rows resembled something out of a Hollywood romance movie. A few rows down on the opposite side, a middle-aged man with a heavy build leaned back in his seat while a woman curled up on his lap, gently stroking his moustache. They spoke in the comfort of each other's arms, breaking their gaze with random hugs, lost in their own world.

In view, over the headrests, a young man stood several rows ahead, gesturing at his seat while smiling and pulling facial expressions. His arms were buried behind the cover of his backrest, yet he looked familiar. I momentarily held my gaze on the man as he conversed with his seat. Even stranger was that none of the passengers alongside him reacted to his odd behaviour. Suddenly, his face registered in my memory; he was the young man pacing back and forth at the top of the stairs, his sidelocks now dangled freely without his Haredi hat. The mystery was further solved when the young man raised his concealed arms, revealing an infant whom he began to hug and kiss.

Speeding along, the plane cut through a cluster of large clouds and encountered turbulence. The crowd was utterly oblivious, deeply engrossed in their conversations. They paid no attention to the bumps, and the turbulence subsided without incident. In an attempt to relax, I filled the confined space with my legs stretched as far as possible, and as the noise quietened, my eyelids grew heavy until everything became silent.

2

Sunday – Welcome to Israel

I woke up disoriented and unfamiliar with my surroundings. However, hearing the pilot's articulate British accent from the speakers restored my bearings and brought me back to my rear-seat view of the cabin.

"Cabin crew, prepare for landing."

The flight attendants sprang into action, patrolling the length of the aisle and performing their landing routines. The lead hostess moved along the rear of the plane with a brisk walk, a trash bag flapping in her left hand while her ring (resembling a wedding ring) glittered under the cabin lights. Excitement had returned to the cabin, and the crew were sailing with it.

As we touched down, a high-pitched cheer and a hail of claps resounded within the dimly lit cabin. This was not a celebration of joining the 75,000 Flights Club, which landed at the Ben Gurion Airport yearly; this was a homecoming celebration. Regardless of where they resided, millions of Ashkenazi, Sephardic and Mizrahi Jews, Sunni Arabs (Arab Israeli) and more make this annual homecoming trip.

The plane pulled into the apron and stopped inside a thick mist, with spots of fluorescent lamps glowing from within. As the celebrations came to a brisk end, the passengers slammed the overhead bins open before they raced through the door.

I threw on my puffer coat and followed the exiting passengers down the aisle onto a jetway. A moist, earthy draught seeped in through an opening in the jetway, reminding me of my trip to Turkey, a country where my lack of native tongue proved to be a significant challenge in navigating.

When we exited the jetway, an Israeli flag hung high on the wall; it was hard to miss. But, like a herd of sheep, the passengers pressed forward through the corridors, disregarding the obscure Hebrew signs.

The leading passengers walked confidently, and the remaining passengers followed without question. I had almost drifted into autopilot when we emerged from a corridor into an open space, where the passengers dispersed like dandelions in the wind. Another Israeli flag hung high on the inside wall, and I sensed a deep spirit of patriotism within the country. The airport was bustling with rapid activity; people, workers, and travellers marched along invisible lines.

As I swept through the maze of corridors, I noticed the presence of armed security stationed at every corner. Though it was common knowledge that Israel had tight security, witnessing it in person was a whole different experience. The armed personnel held the fort, barely breaking their stoic-faced guard. I felt briefly comforted by what appeared to be competent security. However, there was a thin line between adequate state security and a military state, and neither inspired the feeling of exploring with freedom.

When my eyes escaped the claustrophobic passage walls and fell on the internal architecture of the airport hall, I swiftly forgot my security concerns. The view opened to a panoramic grid of Jerusalem stones, masoned with precision. The spherical layout of the walls offered a 360-degree view of the airport from the top floor, robbing my ability to size the space. However, upon further inspection, the airport appeared enormous against the miniature bodies walking below. I gazed through the glass expanse before me, and the airport walls came alive, expanding into the distance. The stone columns stood in a palette of pale sand shades, all polished to a natural finish. The stone walkway formed two long diagonal lines intersecting at the edges, and exiting passengers surrendered to the pull of the slope, staggering along their path with suitcases sliding down with ease like marbles in a playground. I grew impatient, eager to exit the stunning walls.

At the exit, an officer diverted me to an identification area, which I had unknowingly missed on my way down. I queued in a small, designated area in front of three metallic machines resembling robots from Dr Who. My passport was now sitting open and face down on an illuminated glass tray for what felt much longer than the usual five seconds. An electric dual shutter pinged from within the machine, and a piece of paper slid out with a blue pixelated print of my portrait photograph and passenger information. I was unimpressed with the walk back for a piece of paper resembling something from a fortune cookie, slid the document into my passport and returned towards the exit.

I joined the crowd of passengers waiting and was approached shortly after by a dark-skinned man with features of East African descent. He could have been an Abayudaya (Jews mainly from Uganda), an Ethiopian Jew or any of the several African Israelis who are rarely talked about in everyday media but have come to know Israel as home.

"Can I see your passport?"

I hesitated, conscious of the man's lack of a uniform or badge. He repeated the question, this time smiling with a comforting assurance. I handed over my passport, and the man casually flipped through the pages before returning it.

"You may go," he said, pointing towards a space at the exit. The glamour of the airport faded behind my exhaustion from the security process. As with most security-heavy states, the little details, such as customer experience, had been forgotten behind the wall of protection. Fear has always been an inefficient form of security; it affects the perpetrators of harm and the innocent and constantly requires raising stakes and resources.

Approaching the exit, I slipped my passport into the inner pocket of my puffer coat, hoping that would be my last encounter with security. I then caught sight of the words "mobile" and "data" displayed boldly in English among the Hebrew advertising in front of a small kiosk next to the main airport entrance.

Speaking to the attendant, I opted for the eight-day data plan from the available options at the cost of 180 shekels. I had spent ample time checking conversion rates before flying and, with a quick mental calculation, dividing 180 by 4, the £45 felt fair considering the airport rates were premium.

I reached into my pocket, pulled out my phone, and the screen brightened. The time read 7:45 p.m., and the battery showed a measly 14 per cent charge. The attendant was now swapping the SIM card from my phone, which I left with him charging before heading towards the car rental services on the first floor. I walked towards the only illuminated store among the row of offices, where a woman stood barely taller than the desk as the other attendants were circled further back, casually conversing.

"Hello. I'm looking to rent a car."

"Hi. What type of car would you like?"

"Something cheap for a week. I would like to drive to Haifa—"

"That's fine," the woman responded as her talking colleagues lowered their voices.

"Tel Aviv—"

"I can help with that," she continued.

"Bethlehem—"

"Oh, sorry! For insurance reasons, you cannot drive our vehicles to Bethlehem," said the woman. "That is a red zone."

The southern Palestinian town was considered a danger zone and even warned against by some tourist guides. It was likely a national policy and, therefore, not worth checking with other rental companies. The woman presented a business card, circling her contact number at my request while I decided to keep my options open.

Returning in a hurry to the phone kiosk, I paid the attendant in cash, with what felt like a drop in the ocean compared to what I had left in my wallet. However, my deflated wallet in my jeans pocket pleased me that I bought all the available Israeli shekels back in London. I asked the kiosk attendant for travel information, and he pointed to a shop two stalls down, which had a large green and purple sticker of a Rav-Kav card stuck to the closed roller shutters. "That is what you need. You can buy it at most convenience stores," he said.

Outside the airport, the roads glowed from the bright overhead lamps. My first destination was Netanya, located in the Northern Central province of Israel. I planned to join the estimated 200,000 inhabitants for three nights. The region had seen a significant shift in its demographic, having previously been an Arab-dominated region before a large injection of United States-linked funding birthed a new type of local. I required a vehicle for my vaguely planned trip and was now considering alternatives around Israel. Online sources informed me of the restricted parking options in Tel Aviv, so I had intended to stay in Netanya, which was a relatively short drive to Tel Aviv (where my trip ended).

With a quick tap, I unlocked my phone and turned off the aeroplane mode. Instantly, the phone buzzed with vibrating notifications, the time updated to 10:11 p.m., and the battery surged to 40 per cent. Conscious of the time, I made a quick dash for the train station, acquired a single ticket to Netanya (from another machine resembling something from the early 20th century), and caught the last 704 train.

I received another notification: a message from David, the Airbnb host in Netanya, who was listing his room for the first time.

David: "Hello, let me know the time of your arrival. I am waiting for you."

Despite my reply with an ETA of 50 minutes, it was well past my check-in time of 3:00 p.m., and it was a Sunday night — David probably had to work the following day.

The train dashed along the track, leaving the primarily white buildings floating in a trail of vivid, multicoloured neon lights against the backdrop of the dark sky. The spectacle offered a distraction, but this was short-lived, as the pressure of time weighed on me with my phone now down to a 30 per cent charge.

The train crept to an unexpected stop at the city of Herzliya, and with "No further services" displayed on the notification board, the driver ushered us through the exit. Outside, the small group of exiting passengers dwindled swiftly to three people.

I waited vigilantly at the bus stop, and though the road was dim, a partially filled car park metres away was a comforting sight. It was now 11.15 p.m., and apart from David, I had a new concern: keeping my phone running with the rapidly depleting charge. Weighing the situation, I wasted no further time and opened the Uber app, quickly typing David's address. On the app, a short distance away, a taxi hovered with an arrival time of five minutes. The vehicle hovered for a moment before heading towards my location, and when it closed in, looped around in circles while my phone charge slipped to 14 per cent. I immediately reached for the power button, dimming the screen.

In the distance, behind the cover of the trees, a vehicle's headlights brightened the road, bringing a sense of hope. A white car pulled out from the glare and veered right, disappearing into the shade of darkness as silence returned to the area. Shortly after, another vehicle swerved into view, heading towards me. As it closed in, the plate number differed from the app booking. A woman walked down from the station exit, her heels clicking against the tarmac before disappearing into the waiting vehicle. I felt a momentary disappointment and distracted myself with the thought of an alternate Uber booking, but the thought ended at the sight of a sudden flash of light. A vehicle cruised towards me, with its silhouette hiding behind the glare of its headlights; it came to rest at arm's length.

"Hello, trip to Netanya?" asked the driver as he tried to manage his phonology.

"Yes!" I delightedly responded, clambering into the rear seat with my rucksack filling half the space. "You appear to be going around in circles."

"Yes, sorry, my phone location…not work well…this area," said the driver, his tongue prominently rolling as he spoke, enunciating with a deep Arabic cadence.

"Not to worry."

The taxi's interior smelled of stale cigarettes, but I embraced it with gratitude. After checking my phone to find my battery was down to nine per cent, I switched the phone off with a slight relief, but the journey was not yet over. The driver set off, manoeuvring onto the empty, dark motorway, accelerating northbound, giving me a moment of rest.

As we rode, I drifted in and out of sleep until we finally pulled up to the destination. A cluster of buildings stood before me in the darkness of the night, and 280 shekels richer, the driver drove off into the distance. My phone was back on, but now at a five per cent charge. I decided against calling David to conserve my phone power and sent him a message instead.

"I've arrived."

A single grey tick marked the message, and a second grey tick appeared shortly after. I roamed the dark footpaths intertwining the buildings, my shoes patting the slippery pavement. I watched with anticipation as my battery dropped to three per cent. The double-blue tick signalled a sign of hope, but there was no response. I failed to locate the numbers on the buildings in the darkness, so I returned to the front gate, closer to the streetlamps, on the wish of a star, while my phone hung at one per cent.

At the open gate, a muscular figure stood in the shadows, showing no movement. I approached the figure, and the person began walking towards me. We met in the darkness, and the man's facial features were now more visible.

"Hello. You are finally here," said the man.

I had only seen David's face from his Airbnb account, but this had to be him.

"Hello. Yes. Apologies for keeping you up this late."

"Don't worry, I'm glad you made it okay," said David. "This way," he continued, heading upstairs to the third floor, where he pushed open a black metallic door, which abruptly stopped under its weight.

The entrance opened into a house illuminated with warm, incandescent lights. A large, monochrome oil painting of Tel Aviv contrasted against one of the white walls, and in the corner of the living room, on a chest of drawers, a carved wooden instrument perched, resembling a lyre, its strings wrapped around a miniature bow. The familiar Israeli flag tilted over the television, and the small, folded pennant draped over a wooden shelf, housing a white and cream candle that had burnt some way down.

"Welcome to Israel!" said David.

"Thank you. I'm glad to be here."

"Let me show you your room."

I followed David upstairs, and hidden behind a sliding frosted-glass door was a spacious room connected to an ensuite bathroom.

"This is all yours," said David. "You can also help yourself to anything in the fridge."

He left the room, and the sound of a door sliding shut echoed from the lower floor, followed by a tap of a switch, bringing the flat to silence. I sat on the edge of the bed, recounting the day's events and how close I had come to being stranded with a dead phone. I brushed the concerns aside, embracing the bubbling excitement. Destiny was calling, with her voice whispering in the air, and nothing could hinder the purpose of my trip.

The curtains hung open, and outside, the silhouette of the trees stood in perfect stillness against the neighbourhood lights. They appeared alive, watching guard. The night's mystique conjured Amagi to mind but swiftly departed. My rucksack fell as I offloaded it on the concrete floor.

In the darkness, the moon's light bounced off the white walls, covering the room in a serene glow. I lay in the bed next to my charging phone and flat power bank, savouring the silence of the night.

3

Monday – Trip to Haifa

Slowly, I woke up to a cold draught nipping at my exposed feet. I had the sense I was at home in London for a moment, but the sharp, musky scent and the faint sound of cries, barks and horns filtering through the concrete walls told me otherwise. The cool shower cleared the drowsiness, giving me a better appreciation of the room as the daylight filled the bright walls, expanding the space within.

Outside, the flat had transformed; the rough plastered finish gave it a tropical look, and the bright white paint lent a warmth that overshadowed my concerns about the previous night's dingy-looking pathways. A line of palm trees stood tall along the fence while snouts of air conditioners protruded through the walls of the flats, reminding me I was far from Europe. Below the trees, patches of grass exposed the hardened soil, making the concrete sidewalk a more desirable path.

With the flat west of Netanya, the broad plan was to explore the northern region of Israel, move south, and finish my holiday west, nearest to the airport. I headed for the bus stop to begin the first leg of my journey to Haifa. Along the narrow path, a dark-skinned woman sat quietly behind a galvanised tall picket gate. Under her watchful eye, a pack of toddlers played carefree within the premises while a chorus of cries streamed from inside the building. A rusty metal plate displayed the name of what turned out to be a nursery, and just as the woman who watched the toddlers was absent of emotion and indifferent to their cries, the signpost's colours were pale, robbed by the sun's heat.

After a five-minute walk, I reached the bus where two women rested beneath the canopy. I chose to wait for the bus in the sunshine, which would be the first of my two rides. The first trip would take me into

Netanya, where I would board another bus for the 55-minute ride to Haifa. To the pleasure of the two women cooling under the canopy, the bus arrived two minutes early. I boarded the bus and swiped at the reader with my bank card. A loud buzzer left the driver unimpressed; shaking his head, he pointed at the Rav-Kav sign (the same from the airport) plastered to the window before waving me onto the bus. I sat with my camera dangling from my shoulder, staring through the tinted glass; the roads were scanty, the pace slow, and there was a widespread absence of activity among the shops, which were still mostly closed. Then, my attention swivelled to the Rav-Kav card; it was my only means of travelling, and I planned to acquire one.

I hopped off at Netanya bus station, one of the many national interchanges, and scanned the nearby buildings for a convenience store, which left me with no options. At a nearby bus stop, a young woman dressed in an IDF uniform sat browsing her phone. I asked for some information regarding the Rav-Kav, to which she informed me there were no vendors nearby, but just as I turned to leave, she spoke again.

"You don't need it - use this," she said, opening the Moovit phone app.

She confirmed the app worked across Israel, and within seconds, I had it installed on my phone and headed towards the next bus stop. My phone showed it was a five-minute walk to the № 2 motorway. However, gazing down from the flyover intersecting the highway, I failed to find the access point. I eventually joined a group of individuals as they tiptoed along the remnants of an abandoned roadside excavation, which had created a temporary passage at the end of the bridge. The path left a sandy trail onto the concrete pavement, where two adjoining bus shelters shielded commuters from the searing sun. When I joined the pavement, the luggage cabin on a coach was closing, and a man in an IDF uniform had just boarded before the doors closed, and the coach sped off.

The crowd lingered with anticipation, like flamingos, their necks stretched out with their heads bobbing as they waited for their respective coaches. A few feet to my right, among those waiting, was another young man in an IDF uniform. A camouflage backpack lay beside him on the sandy ground while a rifle dangled from his shoulder. He cradled the gun to the indifference of onlookers, carrying out his duty with a steely, youthful face.

Under the raging sun, the city swung into full motion. Vehicles of all sizes zipped back and forth along the motorway, their engines leaving echoes in the air. More people gathered beneath the bus stop, seeking refuge in the sliding shade. In the distance, I could see people walking on the busy sidewalks, and more IDF personnel were visible. The olive-uniformed (ground forces) men and women were popping up everywhere, but their navy and air force counterparts, who commonly wore beige uniforms, were nowhere in sight. The Israel Defence Forces were still going strong after 75 years, aided by the mandated subscription for all citizens, barring some Arab sects, and some individuals on religious and medical grounds.

Another set of coaches swerved into the designated pick-up area, their luggage bays swinging open. The young soldier threw his bag into the lower storage area before boarding the coach, with a continued focus on his rifle as he ascended the narrow steps. His unwavering focus drew my attention; I had observed it as a standard trait, an extension of the army uniform in Israel. The driver wasted no time before the coach zoomed off into the distance.

The waiting passengers grew impatient as the temperature rose with the sun across the clear sky. Moments later, another coach arrived, destined for Haifa. I proudly scanned my Moovit app and felt another rush of giddiness. This moment was another small step towards my destined path, one I refused to anticipate but trusted within myself.

Gazing outside as we rode along the highway, the extended acres of levelled farmland gradually washed into a rugged region of sedimentary sand, gravel, and rocks. The surface gleamed with a pale greyish-beige shine, and tufts of low-sprouting shrubs scattered across the ground. Further out, a line of jagged, rocky hills began to rise, fencing the area.

Some of the passengers slept as the engine revved aloud along the motorway. Forty-five minutes into the journey, the roadside vegetation had built up in thickness and height, encroaching on the road. The traffic was now heavier, and the light sleepers began to wake from the increased noise, joining me in watching the passing landscape, now marked by rolling hills.

As we approached, I recognised the city of Haifa, having seen pictures of it on the internet. Low-hanging clouds drifted into the rise of hills, creating a light mirage. In an unexpected trick of the eye, blocks of elevated apartments along the deep-sloping terrain appeared to vanish and reappear. I gazed at the mirage, and with the horizon hidden, the city felt condensed. Picture a slanted surface with a pile of gigantic oyster shells moulded together by mud, rising to the heavens like an arc; a one-way cave, a visual black hole with no escape.

The thin cypress, the branchy cedar and various palm trees were some of the visible tree species, breathing between the crammed towering towers. At a glance, the buildings, mostly high-rise flats, shimmered with a pale white sheen. The prominence of this faded when pinky-beige buildings began to surface along the inner roads. Elongated European-styled buildings (mainly German with minimalist layouts and uniform small windows) balanced on the slopes of Mount Carmel, like goats on a rock edge, visually defying gravity.

The coach crossed the city's boundaries, and the last sleeping passengers woke to the clamouring noise of vehicles. As we pulled up to the train and bus depot of HaMifrats Central, I saw the arched № 22 motorway ascending towards the cliffs, resembling a highway to heaven. The motorway entrance lacked pedestrian access, so I boarded a train headed west, which shortly terminated at the next stop, Haifa Center (HaShmona) station, where exiting passengers wandered in all directions and spilt onto the nearby roads and sidewalks. The only stationary commuters were a large group of Asian tourists lingering near the entrance, staring at maps.

With the motorway still on my mind, I headed towards HaMifrats Central, hoping to glimpse the city from its viewpoint. Still facing the lack of a footpath, I headed back east. It was unclear what I was in Haifa to accomplish, except for a firm conviction I had to be there: a sense of purpose. As I trod the narrow, uneven tarmac of Natanzon Street, a yacht-like structure floated across the sky. Intrigued, I headed towards the structure, which, on closer inspection, resembled the Burj Al Arab in Dubai and the W Hotel (Hotel Vela) in Barcelona, with a sail-shaped arc running across the height. This was the District Government Center for Haifa, a 27-storey, 137-metre building with black steel loops lining the walkway. I ventured into the deceivingly welcoming entrance, and a band of private security brought my childish curiosity to a brisk, polite end.

The visible towers lining the cliffs appeared European, masking three thousand years of historical development, which now stood as an amalgamation of

German, Roman, Ottoman and religious-infused styles and architectures. Patches of cement over granite, sandstone and cement building blocks stood scattered throughout the lower streets of Haifa.

I had spent most of the day exploring the varying architectural styles of the quiet streets of the business district, shooting photographs in scarcely permitted areas. However, when I suddenly emerged through the Greek Catholic Cemetery onto Plummer Street, I found Haifa Centre (HaShmona) station bustling with people.

As surrounding venues prepared to open, the cement pavements dripped from the recent drizzle and smelled of stale alcoholic beverages, while stacked benches were air-drying under the warming air.

I had drifted into autopilot, following my refined blueprint for navigating any city. It started with the flow of the landscape, which innately dictated the second and final lead: the flow of the inhabitants. My lens now stared at the ground as the camera dangled from my shoulder. I had exhausted all the mental imprints inspiration had to offer and lost my creativity amid a brief moment of mindlessness. My mind traversed the last few turns I had made, pondering if I had missed something, and just before my intrigue whittled, I walked into a crowd. As they dispersed along the high street, I trailed them westward, passing the rusty cargo tanks lining the port tracks.

Standing tall at the end of the buzzing Sderot Ben Gurion Street was the Bahá'í Garden, towering one km above ground level, sitting on Mount Carmel; it was unmissable. With a resurgence of purpose, I headed towards the building and found my way to the discreet metallic fence, where I peeped through the black gate.

From ground level, the 1,500-plus steps appeared to run forever, and guarding them at each landing level were pairs of dwarf palm trees, their branches spread like the wings of angels. Beyond the steps, a structure with a dome-shaped golden roof was nested peacefully. What looked like a government building was, in fact, a set of terraces representing the first disciples of the Bahá'í faith, prophesying the importance of all religions and the unity of people. The main terrace held the shrine of Báb, the burial place of the founder of the Bábí faith.

A perfectly trimmed lawn spread along the premises and the colourful hues of leaves blossoming to the top gave the venue warmth and balance: a welcoming setup.

Staring at the shrine, raised like the golden staff of Moses, I barely noticed the security when I walked through the gate. For a brief moment, I contemplated the allure of the divine steps, trying to quieten the voice in my head, urging me to stick to the plan. However, the truth was that I had no plan and had resorted to my original blueprint, the pressing sentiment. One I trusted over anything else, and the Bahá'í Gardens was not on my current itinerary.

Outside the gate, my phone vibrated with a message from Faaezah, an Arab Israeli who had lived briefly in Haifa and whom I trusted as a local information source. She listed some places to eat out, and Kalamaris (a homograph of my favourite seafood dish), located at the heights of the German colony, stood out. Her message came at the perfect time as my attempts to subdue my rumbling stomach were waning. The air was now hot and faintly humid, making the expected thirty-minute uphill walk gruesome.

In the hope of catching a bus, I trudged uphill with my boots hammering against the hot tarmac. After a few minutes, a bus dashed past, its engine working hard, pushing it up the steep road. I abandoned my idea of catching a bus when the sidewalk began to narrow, vanishing into the tarmac. The right-hand section of the road was topped with bumpy, hardened soil and sectioned off as a narrow sidewalk. I crossed and clung to the edge of the stony footpath, guarded by a weak metal railing running along the side, for which, with every step I walked, the outer ground dropped further away, sliding the skyline into view.

Further up the steep incline, a familiar heavy grinding sound echoed from behind, and another bus soared up the hill and out of sight. The reality of my situation had already set in, and I slowed down to a more sustainable walking pace.

The buildings beneath shrank into small cubes topped with overlapping rooftops. The breeze at this higher altitude whistled through the trees, which dangled loosely from the roadside. As I closed in on my six-hundred-foot-high destination, the roads below looked more like sticks traversed by people resembling insects. The houses along the route were primarily flats, some showing cracks from the pull of the inclination. The architectural styles were consistent, with large blocks glowing from a bare cement coat and the extended white roller blinds and protruding air conditioners failing to brighten the dull look. I eventually reduced my pace to a crawl as vertigo began to kick in.

I reached the destination on the map with no restaurant in sight. However, the line of luxurious vehicles parked along the pavement assured me I was in the right place. Further ahead, I could see the Stella Marie Observatory, a white, corrugated steel, domed structure so named due to its proximity to the Stella

Maris Monastery. The observatory was a popular stop for tourists seeking a panoramic view of Haifa and has been a pivotal site in Israeli history. Facing the Mediterranean, this viewpoint provided a strategic surveillance advantage over invading forces and remained an active naval base.

I walked along the walls of Stella Marie Observatory and unearthed the entrance to Kalamaris, buried behind a wall of shrubs. Though I sought only one type of respite, the tinted windows and delicately illuminated restaurant walls relieved my eyes.

Signalling at the waiter, I wasted no time skipping through the menu. Squinting at the low-contrasted cursive text, I shrugged off the thought of an eye test while another reminder letter sat at the bottom of the bin back in London.

A tall waiter with glossy cinnamon-toned skin and a warm smile approached me. At his prompt, I ordered the house special of calamari and sea bass, my standard order for every first seafood restaurant visit, which made comparisons easy. I acknowledged the waiter with a nod, and as he disappeared towards the ordering desk, another waiter approached, balancing a handful of items. He laid out a basket of flatbread, a plate of olives, a blended spice dip and an empty saucer.

I was impressed with the initial service and secretly admired the waiter's balancing act. After a quick hand wash, I dug in, plunging the torn piece of bread into the spicy dip. The soft, thin crust parted in the middle, and the crumbs broke, releasing a doughy oven scent as the bread crumbled against the base of the sauce, leaving fragments behind. As I bit the drenched, torn bread, my eyes jutted open as the sharp taste kicked in. I rolled an olive over my tongue to soothe the taste, pressing it against my front teeth. The juice dripped, quenching the burn and tickling my nostrils with a light tingle.

The pips began to stack up on the empty plate as the pile of olives shrunk; the breadcrumbs trickled onto the tablecloth, gathering like snowflakes. I drank endless glasses of water to quench my thirst, unleashing a deeper appetite. The waiter dashed to the table at the sight of the empty plate of olives.

With the rage of my hunger subsided, I was now on a roll. I had just finished the last olive when the tall waiter rushed back out.

“Are you ready for your main, sir?”

“Absolutely!”

The waiter swiftly cleared the table before unloading the side basket of calamari, the grilled sea bass, a portion of fried cubed potatoes, and a portion of special house salad accompanied by three sauces.

“What are the extra plates?”

“The potatoes, salads and sauces are on the house, sir.”

The experience was getting better and better. I reached for the quarter lemon and soaked the basket of squid with a tight squeeze. Grabbing the fork, I speared the calamari and soon reduced the basket to an empty vessel filled with more oily crumbs.

My glass cup flashed as the main restaurant door swung open, and an elderly couple strolled in, holding hands. The prematurely fading winter sunlight illuminated the stairs, but the restaurant soon returned to the dimmed lighting, and the seating area started filling with hungry mouths.

The plate of sea bass sat cooling while I garnished a slice of fish with a scoop of the special salad. The bright colours sat perfectly over the soft white chunks, and the delicate mango slices overwhelmed the vegetables. But like a sinking ship, it faded into the corners of my palate. The gentle pinch of crispy lettuce, masked by a sour taste, blended with the seasoned fish and fried potatoes drizzled with tahini sauce, joined the path of no return.

Time passed, and the restaurant was soon packed, with most patrons speaking Arabic and a few, Hebrew. Slowly, the sun crept out of sight, and the restaurant glittered with neon lights around its walls and tables. The tall waiter emerged from behind a pillar to check my progress, once again with a warm smile, peering through a pair of trendy spherical glasses. He spoke eloquently and was jovial; he would have comfortably passed as a Londoner back home. I asked him his name.

"I'm Omar."

"Are you from around here?"

"Yes—I was born here in Haifa and have lived here all my life," he replied. He was one of the estimated 300,000 inhabitants of Haifa and, from his name, one of the 11 per cent of Muslims who comprise some Arab Israelis, Lebanese, and Palestinians.

Haifa was ethnically heterogeneous, and it was now clear that the mosaic of different architecture I had seen on my walk represented the diversity of its inhabitants. I liked Omar, and even though he represented only a small percentage of the inhabitants in Haifa, he gave me a good feeling about the city.

We spoke briefly about life in Haifa before I requested the bill, at which point he topped up my glass of water and cleared the table before escaping into the kitchen with the usual swift response.

Sipping my glass of water, I gazed through the tinted windows. The fading daylight shimmered against the tranquil waves blinking back at me. I suddenly realised that I could be drinking from the desalinated seawater before me. In some stretch of relation, as *we are what we eat*, I was ingesting parts of all the countries lining the sea, pieces of religion, culture and doctrines, all at once.

While the second waiter fiddled with the printer roll at the counter, I was distracted by the intrusion of an engulfing shadow. A body leaned into view with arms stretched out; it was Omar. He whipped out a small tray and placed a steaming chocolate brownie on the table, cupped in baking paper, sitting in a circular cast iron bowl. Next to the brownie, a dollop of vanilla ice cream melted in a small bowl and a lone glass of hot water infused with mint leaves steamed at the edge of the tray. There was a brief silence before we laughed, drawing eyes around the restaurant.

"What's this?! This doesn't look like the bill," I said, chuckling.

"No, it's not – this is on the house, sir,"

"Omar – I don't think there's room for this."

"There's always room…"

"For dessert…" I interrupted. "I know, I know. I'll see what I can do."

"Okay, I hope you like it, sir. Enjoy," said Omar.

I stared inquisitively at the tray, focused on the small crack running along the top surface of the brownie, steaming like a volcano. I scooped the ice cream onto the brownie, and it seeped into it and bubbled like escaping lava. I wasted no time and plunged my spoon in, and the spongy dough caved in before giving way to its inner chocolate filling. More steam escaped as the molten ice cream found new depths, and finally, with a first bite, I nested the spoon on my tongue, letting it sit for a few seconds.

At the counter, Omar watched, patiently waiting for a sign of approval, and I gave a thumbs-up without hesitation.

After paying the bill, I walked over to Omar and thanked him for the service. He expressed his gratitude by acknowledging with a nod.

Outside the restaurant, it was now dark, and from over the Stella Maris observatory, the city lights shone through the darkness, forming a reflective glow on the clouds. At the same time, the sound of the sea washing against the coastline ascended with the wind.

I decided to enjoy the crisp night breeze and walk into the town centre, hoping the sloping streets would provide a relaxing path down. I explored the streets of the German Colony, which had lost the visual representation of the historic Palestine where it was established by German Protestant Templars (not to be mistaken with the Knights Templar).

I gradually headed for the high street. The once-vacant bars and restaurants were now lit in a kaleidoscope of hues. The noise rang out from all directions, and from the view outside the venues, it was almost impossible to identify the cultural or religious affiliations. Though the legal drinking age in Israel was 18, the patrons were mostly older adults, a reflection of the conflict in Israel between liberalism and conservatism. Their clothing, however, told a different story. Compared to the daytime, there were few signs of religious and cultural dress; instead, people flowered in an array of modern-casual styles, invariably rounded off by a pair of jeans. I could have been anywhere in the world.

I felt parched from the spices of the dinner. Scanning the high street, I headed towards a brightly decorated bar. Inside, I ordered a bottle of distilled water for ten shekels, as advertised on the menu board above the bar. While the bartender was busy re-organising the till, I navigated my way towards the seating section, and with most of the tables occupied, I headed deeper. The music was quiet but loud enough to create a cosy ambience under the dim lights. Walking through the compact space, I lightly brushed shoulders with a man in a red jacket, to which he didn't react.

I settled at a small wooden table and began scrolling through my phone looking up the places I intended to visit in Israel. Jerusalem, Tel Aviv, Nazareth, and the West Bank were high on my list. I then began listing the optional venues of the Wailing Wall, Dead Sea, Eilat, and the Golan Heights. I altered the priorities of each destination, for which there was no formula and marked them as my mind led, factoring in logistics. Lost in the glare of my phone, I was oblivious to a voice from the table to my right. The soft, high-pitched voice spoke again.

"You look quite serious! What are you writing?" asked the woman.

I looked over at a woman sitting with her legs crossed. She had dark, curly hair and narrow shoulders; a black metallic ring hung from her nose while her eyes twinkled under the soft lighting.

"Hi. I'm just planning the rest of my trip."

"Are you not from here?"

"No, I'm not. I'm visiting from the UK."

"I've always wanted to visit the UK."

"I recommend visiting, but I cannot promise the same weather you have here."

She introduced herself as Hava, and we continued with small talk. Slender arms draped through the opening of her silky vest, her eyes fluttered, lashes protruding like the cilia of a Venus flytrap. Indeed, those eyes must have entrapped many men.

As we discussed some recommendations for the evening, a man joined the table, the same man I'd bumped into earlier, now holding two drinks. They shared a brief kiss, after which he remained dead silent, yet with a calmly inquisitive smile. The woman turned, continuing the conversation with me before casually extending an invite to a private Aahz party.

This invitation would have come as no surprise if we were in London. Though I was distantly well informed of such secret parties and saucy marathon escapades, I was very aware of the polarising cultural norms in Israel. I chuckled and politely declined, requesting a less colourful option.

"If you are looking for something less colourful, as you so nicely said, you've come to Haifa on the wrong day of the week. Wednesdays are the best party nights. I recommend visiting the Sleek Bar."

The couple vanished into the darkness of the bar, joining a group of friends. I liked the sound of the new recommendation and added it to my list as I strained my eyes under the brightness of my phone.

I downed the rest of my water and pushed towards the exit; the bar was now less crowded, and the couple were nowhere to be seen. Once outside, I walked towards the end of the high street, ready to call it a night.

4
Monday – Hell Ride

While browsing my phone, I walked up to the end of the high street, where the road lights and noise had faded into the distance, and the evening had sharply turned chilly. Inwardly, however, I felt a warmth from the day's events.

From where I stood, the Bahá'í Garden illuminated Mount Carmel with a commanding presence; it was difficult to escape its pull. But this was no mystical inner lead but merely an explorer's desire. I considered staying in Haifa instead of taking a taxi back to Netanya. I left the decision down to the cost of a room in Haifa. If the room cost the same as my taxi ride, it was worth staying to visit the Bahá'í

Garden. At the very least, I needed a taxi to either take me back to the German Colony for the night or to make the trip back to Netanya.

Fortunately, I came across a lone taxi parked on the opposite side of the road with the driver's door open and the windows slightly unwound. The service dome light lit in yellow, and the imprinted word taxi reflected off the glossy white roof.

Inside, a man sat under the faint light in the driver's seat, fiddling nervously with the dashboard. I approached and inquired about the price of a ride to Netanya, to which he responded that it would cost 300 shekels. I began browsing on my phone for nearby hotels in the German Colony to compare prices and asked the driver to give me a moment while I confirmed my destination. He invited me to sit while I browsed, but shortly after I climbed in, he slammed his door shut and accelerated onto the main road, slipping the tyres into a short skid.

"Wait a moment!"

"Yes, yes, we go quick," the driver said, pressing his foot on the accelerator.

"Where are you going? I asked you to wait!"

Paying no attention, he drove on and circled a small roundabout before screeching onto the highway, picking up speed as the engine revved louder. The tyres skidded along the tarmac of the barren motorway as air gushed in through the open windows. The howling of the draught blended over the engine's noise, had left me no choice but to raise my voice louder. The tension grew as an unpleasant taxi ride flooded into my memory. The event occurred in my younger years, back in London, when a male driver tried to get too familiar. He had height and mass over my then-scrawny teenage frame, but this situation was the opposite, and I had left any tolerance for unruly drivers behind years ago.

Silence. The driver was leaning into the steering wheel, shoulders caved in, his eyes glued to the road.

"Hey! Are you hearing what I'm telling you?!" I shouted, my voice rising with frustration as the driver remained unresponsive. "I said wait!"

"No, no, we go quick!"

We argued as my words got lost in translation while the vehicle sped along the widened highway, now onto a triple-lane road. The streetlamps dashed past, forming a tall mirage resembling the Berlin Wall, but soon faded into darkness as the row of lights ended, and the vehicle's headlights beamed against the bare asphalt.

"You kal, gaiit address, we go!" yelled the driver, turning to face me as his chipped, stained teeth gave way to a breath laced with stale cigarette. His head bobbed up and down, dangling on his skinny figure, which became more animated the faster he drove.

I fell silent, my fingers tightening around my phone as adrenaline ran through me. With my focus entirely on the driver, I held back my fist from jerking towards him, but I was losing the struggle. An image of us brawling in the car seat flashed through my mind, and I allowed the thought to run; it felt strangely relaxing. When my focus drifted back to the driver, he was still ranting aloud, now mixed with Hebrew. I had known Israelis to be quite bold, but this driver appeared either on drugs or out of his mind. Nevertheless, I considered my holiday plans, and spending a few nights in a cell was not on my list.

I felt my grip loosen as my arm sank back into my lap, and then I addressed the driver.

"What do you think you are doing?" I yelled at him.

"We go Netan–"

"No, we are not going anywhere. Now, take me back to where you picked me up." I said, staring at the driver. "Now!"

The driver reluctantly slowed the vehicle down and headed towards the nearest exit while he continued to rant in Hebrew. The streetlamps reappeared as we returned towards Haifa, and the illumination eased the tension. The driver finally stopped alongside a man waiting by the roadside and leant out of the window to speak with him in Hebrew. The man climbed into the backseat, and the conversation continued as the driver drove on.

"Hello," greeted the man. "The taxi driver said he wants to take you to Netanya."

"No, the only place he is taking me is where he picked me up."

The man and the driver conversed again in Hebrew. "He said you wasted his time, and he wants money."

"He wants money? He won't be getting a dime from me," I said, staring at the driver.

The man conversed again with the driver, who began shouting. We were getting nowhere, so I pointed at a police station at the opposite end of the road and asked the man in the rear seat (now our translator) to offer the driver the option to resolve the situation with the police. I heard the word "police" among the words of Hebrew, and instantly, the driver's shoulders dropped. I stepped out of the vehicle with the translator to record the vehicle's plate number, and after recording only three characters, the tyres skidded as the driver drove off, showering us with gravel.

"Are they all like this?" I asked the translator.

"No, this one is crazy."

The night was getting colder, and Netanya was now the only option on my mind. I thanked the man for his assistance and informed him of my plans to arrange another taxi to Netanya.

“I’m afraid you won’t find any taxis around here,” he said before dialling a number on his phone and, after 3 minutes, ending the call. “Your taxi should be here in the next five minutes.” He kindly offered to wait until the taxi arrived.

“Are you from Haifa?” I asked.

“No, I’m Ukrainian, but I have lived here most of my life.”

“Good to know. What is your name?”

“Mykhailo.”

As we conversed on the roadside of a dual-carriage lane, my eyes wandered back to Mykhailo while he spoke; I had been briefly distracted. Over his shoulder, Mount Carmel hunched over in the darkness, the lining of the rise imprinted a blackness over the night sky; it was captivating. The phrase “Blacker than black” came to mind, and I named the place “Nigrior niger”. As the thought settled in my mind, Mykhailo's face illuminated like an angel, flashing twice. I realised the light was coming from behind me and turned to see a vehicle racing towards us, with lights flashing and horns honking. It was the driver from earlier, he yelled and gestured with his fingers as he drove past. I took the opportunity to memorise the remaining characters of his plate number.

"I should have gone to the police station."

"That won't help; the police here are pretty useless," said Mykhailo.

After five minutes, a white SUV cruised up to us, and a short man stepped out, asking for the passenger travelling to Netanya. He informed us that the trip would cost 250 shekels. I shook hands with Mykhailo, thanked him, and boarded the taxi while he vanished down a side road.

"My name is Ben," the driver said, adjusting his glasses. "I heard about your previous ride. I'm sorry that happened."

"Thank you, Ben, but these things happen."

Ben was a student studying at university. He reminded me of Omar but with a calmer demeanour.

As we made the fifty-minute journey south, we spoke, and just as I had almost ticked Haifa on my to-do list, he repeated words I had heard earlier in the night.

"You should come on a Wednesday. That's the best night."

There it was. Haifa had found its way back on my list. I had to see what all the fuss was about.

Hanging on to Ben's voice, I summoned the focus to stay awake, drifting in and out of light sleep. We arrived in Netanya, and a handful of shekels later, Ben was gone.

5

Tuesday – The Quiet Shores of Netanya

It was nearly 8:00 a.m. when I woke to chirping birds outside. I felt the cool, crisp air against my face, and my skin prickled as the exposed duvet slid against my bare skin. The city was now awake, and the evidence bared itself in the muffled chorus of vehicles driving back and forth on the distant highway.

I reached for my phone, which had started vibrating and was edging sideways on the table. I skimmed over the list of messages, and one from Faaezah caught my attention.

"Morning. I hope you enjoyed your first day in Israel. If you are still in Netanya, I am free today and can meet you later."

I responded to her message, thanking her for the dining recommendations before informing her I was headed towards the town centre and would be free to meet.

Outside, I was beginning to feel at home. The sounds of screaming toddlers, the barking of dogs and the echoing of distant vehicles were now all elements of the city I recognised.

I headed towards the town centre near the beachfront, hoping to visit the Victory Monument, a WWII memorial marking the victory over the Nazis, with a sculpture resembling an archangel flying through the earth's crust. I navigated through a maze of isolated footpaths, continually veering in different directions. The paths eventually trickled into wide roads with washed-out markings printed over the cracked surface. The footpaths edged along a stretch of bungalows, which lacked a uniform exterior except for the oxblood terracotta roof tiles and large rectangular grey air conditioners protruding from walls commonly coloured in blueish-grey or the same pinkish-beige found in Haifa. Low brick walls with metal fenced poles marked the borders of the homes, and a line of varying grown trees covered the walls from the outside.

After emerging from the network of footpaths, a flat landscape opened up, and distant buildings stood along the horizon. I headed towards the structures along HaAri Street. The road rose into an overhead bridge, and more concrete towers closed in. There was a surprising serenity to the buildings; the first set stood in a row of three, which felt symbolic, and for a moment, I forgot about the searing heat as the lines of sweat trickled down my face.

Twenty minutes later, Faeezah messaged me to confirm that she had finished her work. After arranging to meet on the bridge, I headed east towards the bridge's entrance.

My phone rang half an hour later; Faaezah had reached the bridge and was waiting in traffic. I approached a white vehicle angled towards the curb from the queue line, barely recognising the lightly tanned face sitting in the front seat. It had been two years since we had seen each other in London, where we met at an event of a small group of hosts and travellers. After that, we kept in touch via social media.

I closed the door on the invading heat to find comfort in the air-conditioned space. The built-up traffic dispersed at the sign of the green light, and Faaezah set off toward the coast and headed for the beach.

As we approached the seaside, the streets fell into a spread of shade created by the greyish-blue towers that had now obscured the sun.

After several failed attempts, Faaezah eventually found a parking space on the corner of a side street. She was cautious about the parking restrictions in Netanya and confirmed the rules on a signpost.

"I think we should be good here," said Faaezah.

"Are you sure you don't want to drive the block one last time?" I mocked, which left Faaezah chuckling.

The beachfront presented a perfect location for a catch-up, and as we walked along Ussishkin Street, I had a sweeping view of the area. As we headed south, the footpath rose above the beach, revealing a sparse growth of tall palm trees nested within circular openings on the brick pavement. Further back from the trees, a low concrete fence ran along the stretch of the beach, opening to the sand every hundred metres.

As we gained height, the beach opened up further. The creamy sand stretched towards the sea, and just before the waterline, a forest of blue-topped umbrellas and wooden chairs studded the sand. A few resting bottoms pressed against the seats, and a small group padded along the sand barefooted. I was briefly distracted by a sudden rustle among the nearby shrubs of plants, and the sight of a long, slender, brown, furry tail disappeared beneath the growth, leaving stillness. Moving on, we headed further south.

We later arrived at Matityahu Dankner Street, which stood over seventy feet above the beach below. We came to rest on a wooden side bench with my camera placed to my right, and while we spoke, an elderly couple approached. I watched as the man addressed Faaezah in Hebrew, smiling as they conversed, while the woman stood a few steps behind. As they prepared to leave, the man turned to me.

"I hope you are enjoying the view. If you wait another 30 minutes," the man pointed towards the sea, "the sun will be over the horizon, and you can watch it set."

I thanked him, and the couple left, walking south. As Faaezah and I continued to catch up, time appeared to freeze. The clouds hovered at the edge of the clear sky, and suddenly, like a star performer, the sun took centre stage over the horizon, gliding into view.

I had seen a million sunsets, but this was different; the Mediterranean stretched towards the horizon, dressed in a perfect pattern of even ripples. The sun floated at arm's reach, so close it felt you could almost touch it. A light haze of cloud left the glow visible; you could practically see its flames breathing. We gazed quietly at the horizon as the sun slowly disappeared. But once the show was over and the sun was out of sight, the novelty of the silence was lost. I named the place "Prope ad solem", where I almost touched the sun.

We decided to go and eat and walked towards the car. As we prepared to leave the footpath, a large brown mongoose appeared and perched on a concrete slab surrounded by a clowder of cats. Its furry tail (the same one from the rustling shrubs) was sprung, ready to pounce. There was a sudden loud bark in the distance, and the tension rapidly subsided into an anti-climax as the cats scattered out of sight. The moment felt symbolic, and I kept a mental register.

The clear sky had begun to darken, and the streetlamps flickered on. We bypassed the car and walked to the Netanya City Market. The area was buzzing, and most of the patrons were women, a noticeable number dressed in Arab clothing as they selected among a splendour of exotic fruits and heaps of organised dried nuts and grains. Ama-gi crossed my mind. Though not a woman of faith, she was well-versed in most local customs and religious practices. Her tunic, covered with a body-length scarf, which often concealed her forehead and hair, exposing the pale olive skin of her face, allowed her the camouflage of a local. The exclusive witnesses of her dark auburn hair nicknamed her "elah [terebinth]" after the tree, with its red blossomed flowers, commonly found around Jerusalem and Palestine.

Unable to find a restaurant to complement our appetite, we returned to the car, making a short pitstop at a bakery. There was euphoria among the attendants as their lips synced to the lyrics of a Hebrew song ripping through the speakers. I picked a handful of pastries, and at the checkout, the attendant topped up my bag with complimentary doughnuts. She followed the gift with the words, "Happy Hanukkah!" I had heard the word Hanukkah but had never addressed it directly. It was the celebration of the menorah, which burnt in the temple of the recaptured Jerusalem for a miraculous eight days. This information felt meaningful, but only time would reveal why.

On the road, with hunger burning in our bellies, Faaezah floored the pedal, and we raced north. She swerved through the busy motorway as the tarmac flashed under moving headlights. Faaezah had been driving for five minutes in silence, her eyes fixed on the road, locked in deep thought, before she suddenly spoke.

"I know where to take you!" she exclaimed with excitement in her eyes. She squeezed her little feet against the pedal, and the hybrid engine churned out torque as the car accelerated, manoeuvring across the lanes. She drove up the busy motorway for another thirty minutes and eventually arrived at a dark street, closed in by a stone-mounted wall. A long queue of vehicles lined the tightly parked pavement edge.

We walked the dimly lit pavement, which opened into a bay tiled with long wooden planks and illuminated with fluorescent lighting. The rhythmic sound of bumping boats echoed from the darkness of the water, with the faintly glowing bows bobbing along the dock.

Faaezah led the way towards a row of restaurants before walking into a venue where we sat outside under a large canopy. She offered to order, glanced briefly at the menu and engaged in a fragmented Hebrew exchange with the waitress, who nodded with approval before hurrying away with the menu. Mission accomplished, Faaezah leaned into her chair.

"So, how's work?" I asked.

"It's quite busy – hectic," said Faaezah.

"Dealing with all those toddlers must be," I joked. "Waiting on yours now."

There was a brief silence as Faaezah drifted into deep thought.

"I don't know – I don't think I want to bring a child into this world," she said.

I watched her eyes flicker. My conversations with her were usually a game of cat and mouse. She frequently spoke with overt undertones and unconscious satire. I made a habit of trying to decipher her unspoken words.

"Why is that?"

"There's just so much to deal with as a child in this modern era."

"I can see why you would think that," I responded, "but kids usually sort themselves out."

Contrary to my words of hope, I understood her sentiments. As a paediatrician, she probably had seen it all where children were concerned. However, I also sensed a political undertone; she had experienced hostility during the recent unrest.

At that moment, and for the first time, I realised that in the four years I had known Faaezah, I had never seen her hair, not even a wisp of it. I was impressed with how she always kept it tightly concealed, wrapped in various scarves. That was precisely why, a week prior, I found myself at Ishvari in Stratford Westfield shopping centre trying to buy a scarf.

"Besides, I have to find a husband to make the baby with," Faaezah smiled as her gaze softened.

"I'm sure he's out there somewhere. You will find him in due course."

"God willing," she responded.

Remnants of my binged Arabic TV series flooded my mind, and I heard the word "Inshallah [If God wills]" in my mind's ear.

The waiter interrupted the conversation, dressing the table with various dishes. We wasted no time and began eating, sharing the assortment comprising Israeli salad, steamed peppers, lamb skewers, fragrant rice, pitta bread, and a nosh of seven sauces. We weren't alone; the aroma of the seasoned dishes drew in the roaming cats as they picked at the droppings from the table. We made quick work of the meal, and the cats, with their hungry eyes, migrated to another table.

The harbour was empty, and the sound of the clanging boats failed to restore the sense of human activity. It was the same on the road; with the traffic clear, Faaezah made the most of the free road and dashed along the motorway. The streetlamps flickered as they disappeared out of view, and with a slight stretch and a quick flick of her fingers, cool air seeped into the vehicle as the windows slid open and closed again (something she did every five minutes).

We reached Netanya thirty minutes later, and Faaezah dropped me off. Then, as her headlights speared into the night, she left me in darkness.

Upstairs, David was watching football. It was my last day at his apartment, so I decided to spend some time with him, giving an update on my day and discussing my plans.

"At some point, I plan on travelling to the West Bank. If our plans coincide, I might also meet a friend."

"Where is your friend?" asked David.

"Tel Aviv. He will most likely be there towards the end of the week."

"Where is he from?"

"He's Palestinian… I suspect," I said as David's eyes widened, perking up in his chair. "He's a bit of a ghost – aloof."

"Palestinian?!"

"Yes, though he has never clearly said so."

"No, no, no, he can't be. Here in Israel? No, you mean Arab Israeli?"

"Yes," I responded.

Not versed in political etiquette or the complexities of Israeli society, I politely swayed the conversation away from the subject.

"If you go to the border, be careful – and never look at a Palestinian woman in the face."

"Why is that?" I asked.

"If she is married, it is a major transgression. You could get her killed!"

"Thanks, I'll keep it in mind," I said, inwardly intrigued. "I will end my trip in Tel Aviv."

"Oh, Tel Aviv, the most beautiful women!" said David, kissing the tips of his right-hand fingers.

"So I've heard. Let's hope it's true," I said as we laughed.

I said goodnight, thanked David for hosting me, and headed to my room. On my way up, I reflected on what David said about Palestinian women. Although it had sounded absurd, I recalled a report I'd read of 69 femicides in Israel and the Palestinian territories between 2020 and 2022, 24 of which had fallen victim to their partners or relatives, overall resulting in a split of 29 Jewish-Israeli and 40 Palestinian women losing their lives to domestic violence. There was definitely fire behind the smoke. With Ama-gi, this was a first-hand experience. She had lost a co-worker who was like a sister to similar incidents, and even stranger was the fact that it occurred in their line of work.

The calmness of the night recharged me. I was ready to return to Haifa, but something else was in store on this trip. I called it a night as excitement bubbled in the darkness.

6

Wednesday – Return to Haifa

The house keys clattered on the dining table, and the heavy door slammed shut. I was returning north to the third largest city in Israel, and my feet would once again roam the German Colony. Haifa awaited, but this time, I was making a detour. The sky was saturated with light clouds and looked to be darkening.

I opted for a route change and headed for the Netanya train station. I rode the № 136 train for about an hour before crawling up to a busy platform at the Haifa Central Station. This was familiar ground, and without a second thought, I boarded a bus headed towards the German Colony. The bus rambled through the tight, vibrant streets, elevating with each spin of the wheels.

I was tracking my route with my phone navigator. At the vibration of a notification, I exited the bus. I plodded down one of the side streets to arrive at my pre-booked hotel. This was no fancy stop. It was the bare minimum, a place to rest for the night.

My rucksack dropped onto a thick red Egyptian rug in the confines of the box I called a room, and with a new spring in my step, I headed back outside and caught a bus heading towards the lower central region of the city.

At the central bus station, an inter-city bus was loading a group of eager passengers, pushing to find shelter as the clouds above thickened to a deep shade and spits of rain pelted down.

We drove along Highway № 75, where the temperature dropped, and a light drizzle ensued. Stretches of level green terrain whisked by, giving a glimpse of my awaited destination. I drifted into a reverie, watching the rain spatter against the windows and trickle into patterned veins.

I received another navigation message, completing the first phase of my detour in just over an hour; I was in Nazareth. One of Israel's most significant religious and political cities, the celebrated birthplace and childhood town of Jesus attracted thousands of pilgrims annually. Labelled the "Arab capital of Israel," the inhabitants are 69 per cent Muslim and 30 per cent Christian. It was the fertile ground on which the seeds of Palestinian nationalism (civic and ethnic) flourished.

The coach stopped, and all the passengers disembarked, heading for the nearest shelter. The area was quiet, and the falling rain failed to upset the unexpected serenity. Time slowed to a still; Nazareth appeared to have its own pace. Under the bus shelter, the waiting passengers showed no anticipation as they stared into the rain.

After waiting for thirty minutes, a bus arrived. With a carriage full of crammed passengers, we rode towards the Catholic Church of the Annunciation, which was said to mark where Mary was visited by the angel Gabriel, who informed her she would give birth to Jesus.

The neighbouring buildings edged closer on the tightening strip as the bus rode down the steep, bumpy road. The landscape was undulated in all directions, only visible by the buildings' varying heights, which appeared to lean against each other, masking a mosaic of aesthetic styles (Roman and Ottoman). From silicate bricks to a rough cement finish, the buildings rarely exceeded four storeys high, the building grounds overlapped into confined communal spaces, and the walls appeared dampened from the rain, giving off a dust-stained look. The roads below weaved between the buildings, barely visible from a distance.

As we descended to the bottom of the road, the buildings clustered more tightly, and the lack of pavements made orientation difficult. I eventually found the church's signpost hidden among various information boards.

Outside the gate, a group of tourists stood attentively, listening to the loud voice of their tour guide. Some appeared lost, needing help understanding the English words, and turned to others for guidance. The structure resembled most Roman-style churches. A hollow stillness welcomed me into the sanctum when I walked through the large wooden doors. My first impressions of the city left little to be desired, but the atmosphere in the church was a welcome surprise.

I nestled next to a group of worshippers on the same bench as they prepared to pray. Further down towards the altar, another group of tourists stood taking photographs. The balance of faith and commerce failed to deter us from praying, and like light and darkness, their boundaries remained intact. The atmosphere aroused a feeling of sacredness in me. Authentic or staged, it appeared to work. The last rays of sunlight escaped through the massed clouds, and the stained ceiling windows dimmed inside the church. The building's dark concrete beams absorbed the remaining light.

Shortly after leaving, I strayed from the church and veered into a disappearing sidewalk, stopping next to a small wooden kiosk stacked with pomegranates. The congested kiosk held a transparent plastic jug sloshing with blood-red juice. I was mesmerised by the richness of the colouring among the wrath of swirling white piths. The realisation was humorous, discovering that my frequently ordered 100 per cent pure pomegranate juice, back home, was diluted. I bought a cup of juice and walked along an ascending pathway. With my thoughts still firing away, Ama-gi came to mind. I could see tufts of her hair draping like a curtain pressed beneath the shelter of her scarf. In the searing sun, her hair crispened to a shiny brass maroon tint. Ama-gi was not there in Nazareth, but for a period, it was home. Walking the streets, I felt a deep connection with her and decided to visit a place she would have worked. However, my earlier online search for brothels in Nazareth returned no prospects. The city had seen a crackdown on such activities, with the underground bars and clubs being the primary target of spontaneous police raids. Ama-gi was a woman of the night, but she was too savvy to be caught napping and kept a strict referral-only system when tending to patrons.

Lost in thought, I had drifted into the labyrinth of a network of walkways connecting Old Market Nazareth. The clouds condensed, the skies darkened earlier than expected, and another drizzle ensued. I walked down Al-Bishara Street, ready to return to Haifa, and passed the Greek Catholic Church of Annunciation. I observed the arid ground and thought it implausible that an active spring channel flowed beneath the south-facing structure.

I caught an empty bus headed to Haifa, and just as it pulled off in the heavy rain, the driver slammed on the brakes. I gripped the headrest in front of me just before I slid off the seat. Now more audible, the driver had turned backwards, yelling with hands still on the steering wheel. His words were lost in translation as he shouted in Hebrew. In response to the driver's tone of distress, I rushed towards him.

"Is everything okay?" I asked.

He raised his voice louder under the intensifying raindrops, clattering loudly against the roof and pointed towards the front door, which had just swivelled open. The heavy clattering of rain filled the bus, muffling the driver's voice. He raised his voice even louder with a deeper tone of distress. It was then I placed my cup on the dashboard and peeped outside towards the rear of the bus.

Outside, a wheelchair rolled off the side of the bus while a man dangled from the handle of the central door frame. I rushed to grab him by the shoulders and pulled him onto the bus, seating him near the window. He pointed outside at his wheelchair, throwing his arms towards the storage under the bus, so I headed back outside and folded the wheelchair before I stowed it in the luggage bin.

I climbed onto the bus and heard "Toda raba [Thank you very much]", instinctively responding, "You're welcome".

But why? I had never, up until this point, heard those words. But I probably had, among all the noise at the airport or in passing on the streets. The natural human adaptation was in process; a few days in, it had begun.

When I returned to Haifa, I confined myself to my room, escaping the downpour outside. I was still holding on to the cup of pomegranate juice, which was now empty and quickly found a new home in the bin.

After a warm power nap and a quick shower, I quickly forgot the memories of the damp evening. Dressed in a fresh shirt, I headed for Sleek Bar, the venue Hava had recommended. When I arrived at HaNissi Boulevard, the street was dark with no sign of life, and presuming I had the wrong address, I consulted my phone map, which indicated I had passed the bar. I retraced my steps, halting at the sound of voices nearby. Suddenly, a gaggle of laughter rang out a few blocks down as a bunch of women walked into view before disappearing down a dark entrance, their heels clacked against the ground. I tailed the voices, and as I approached the entrance, a low base reverberated through the walls. I followed the sound into a labyrinth of turns before ending up in a hall where an armed security guard stood at the head of a short queue.

Past the ID verification desk, patrons swarmed the waiting area smoking. Behind the smoking area was the bar entrance, draped with a thick translucent curtain. I blinked as the curtain swiped my face, opening my eyes to the instant change in the ambience. Soft, warm lights illuminated a busy room, revellers covered the central bar, and the DJ was staged in a designated corner on the right-hand side.

I sat at one of the side tables, which gave me a view of the entire bar. The music was familiar but distinct, with hip-hop beats blending melodic Hebrew vocals. With the thundering base ever present, the DJ spun away, and the crowd roared. At the pinnacle of the night, the dining patrons abandoned their partially finished plates and pushed aside their tables to create a restricted, temporary dance floor. The women gathered, swaying their hips while most men watched or danced around the bar. There was an invisible force separating the men and women. Liberal and free, yet the unspoken customs permeated the space. As always, nature had the final say. The men glanced at the women while, in return, in the act of unconscious group participation, the women stretched their arms further out, swaying their hips in ever wider arcs. Eyes met across the distance of the open space. But like a spark, the moment disappeared, and the beautiful dance of life continued.

There was a moment of silence when the music stopped, and suddenly, the sound of a scratching record tore through the speakers before the DJ pulled the song back to the beginning. The silence erupted into a loud cheer, and more people joined the dance floor, their hands waving as they glided to the music. Their stylish outfits failed to hold the dancers back as their arms extended, forming a forest of limbs.

I had no idea what the lyrics meant, but the melody and rhythm spoke a million words. I enjoyed a drink standing among the crowd and conversed with some revellers, receiving an invite to a cafe in Jerusalem run by one of the couples.

The crowd enjoyed the blend of hip-hop and Hebrew with a flare of Middle Eastern routines and body movements, from belly dancing to body popping; it was all present. A series of songs beamed through the speakers, and the chatter spread as the drinks poured from the bar. I finished my drink and decided to call time on a pleasurable night.

I arrived at the hotel just after midnight and reflected on the eventful evening. Haifa did have more to offer, and the return was worth it. But it was on to the next journey, one of the major stops on my list – Jerusalem. I had kept my mind open about what to expect, but I felt it would be pivotal to my trip.

7

Thursday – Whispers in Jerusalem

When I woke up, my head pulsated with a hollowness that made me faintly nauseous. The noise of a roaring engine lent a brief comfort in becoming aware of my surroundings until I peeked outside. Staring back at me were the barren depths of a rocky gorge. The coach rose along the steep road until we pulled into a coach station, where I heard the word "Shalayim" as the driver announced in Hebrew that we had arrived in Jerusalem, one of the oldest cities in the world and the altar to all three major Abrahamic faiths.

A lean, bearded man jumped onto the road, weaving and murmuring through the heavy traffic as his black velvet fedora bobbed up and down. A bus pulled to the stop beside me, and the doors flung open. A gang of teenagers leapt out, spilling onto the sidewalk and taunting each other before dissolving into the whirling crowd. I then boarded a bus that rode the length of Agripas Street, where the intersection was mobbed by a crowd of pedestrians, slowing the traffic to a crawl. Among the crowd was a familiar flickering of dark colours, the widely worn black frock coats made of silk or polyester fabric, and hats of textured mink reserved for married men. Hasidic and Haredi Jews primarily wore these outfits and looking at the black dabs in the market area, there were more than I had seen in Israel.

The sun beat against the ground, and the crowd's feet stamped like an exodus, moving fast against the searing concrete. The sky was a clear, light blue, the perfect backdrop for this timeless scene. There was a rhythm to the city, inaudible but sensed, invisible but felt, and yet everything and every person moved to.

Disembarking the bus, I walked along Jaffa Street, cutting through a side road to avoid the congestion, and arrived at the hostel I had reserved. The chirpy receptionist was British; he had lived in Israel for two years and now called it home.

Clutching my access cards, I navigated through a maze of locked doors strapped beneath the weight of my rucksack, and with the afternoon heat at its peak, I ditched my puffer coat for my light jacket. It was time for my first detour, and I had to make the most of the remaining short daylight hours. I headed towards the Armenian Quarter (part of the walled old city) and skipped exploring the 126,000 square metre enclosure to save time. Instead, I stopped near the Statue of David, off the № 60 motorway, where the late afternoon traffic was now in full swing.

The buses cruised to the stops filled with passengers, leaving no room for those attempting to board. With only a few buses stopping, disappointment swiftly turned to impatience. Like lions chasing their prey, waiting passengers dashed back and forth frantically in search of boarding space.

I joined a group of commuters scampering onto bus № 468. Inside, the bus was bare and lacked modern electronic gadgets. In the absence of a scanner, I abandoned the Moovit app and rummaged through my pockets for change.

The general mood I experienced in Jerusalem was a contagious elation. However, when I settled on the bus, I sensed an immediate change in the atmosphere. The passengers' eyes seeped with deep suspicion, their breathing was bridged with frequent sighs, and the atmosphere was still, on the edge of tension. My excitement took a back seat, realising nobody else shared the feeling. The voice of Bobbie, a close friend, drifted to mind. The conversation from a week prior advised against a visit to the West Bank, which sounded prudent at that very moment. But here I was, on a bus rammed with Palestinians travelling towards the border, and there was no turning back. I had experienced several spikes of inspiration in Israel, short bursts which manifested in the form of impulses and quiet words. However, Jerusalem was an avalanche compared to anything I had felt before. They were so potent that I could almost hear them audibly; I called them whispers, and they had quietened my worries about the West Bank, leaving the flaming impulse to burn wild.

The concerns my friend had were valid. Israel's current prime minister, Yair Lapid, had held office for five months as leader of an interim government. With the results of the recent election handing the baton to the opposition in an unprecedented five elections at the Knesset (the single legislative body of Israel) in four years, the right-wing Likud leader, Benjamin Netanyahu, was set to regain the seat of prime minister. This assignment had come in a year fraught with several protests in Israel. With the Israeli government in control of 60 per cent of the West Bank, a Palestinian territory, things were always on edge in the region.

The passengers stood still like planks of wood, in a collective hypnotic look of exhaustion. I sensed an unease, and my gaze roamed the bus, trying to find a landing place. Sitting to my near left, a man stared into oblivion, shoulders low, face hardened from the pressures of life. Sitting to his right, crouching with his elbows resting on his knees, a boy watched a YouTube video on his phone. With his interest lacking, the entertainment seeped down a black hole as his eyelids struggled to stay open. In the front section of the bus, sitting behind the driver, facing backwards, a woman escaped the squeeze by turning towards the window. Her oversized, black sunglasses concealed her eyes, but her body betrayed the disguise as it softly rested in a contorted position. Most of the men onboard had a medium tan to their skin, with straight black hair running down into a beard. And for the women, some wore their dark, wavy hair free while most wrapped themselves in scarves or hijabs.

The man sitting next to the boy momentarily dropped his head, leaving his neck exposed. Under the cover of his worn denim jacket collar, perching like a snake in the grass, the edge of a scarf ran across the base of his neck. It was no ordinary scarf, but a shemagh (keffiyeh or kufiyyeh), a commonly worn scarf by Middle Eastern men, which offers both protection from the heat and stands as a traditional fashion emblem. The cotton fabric comes woven in various colours. However, the black and white square patterned fabric, which was visible within the shade of his neck, was an iconic symbol of Palestinian solidarity, especially during protests and military combat.

Like a ride to a funeral, silence rang loud through the cramped space before a gradual shift in atmosphere left the passengers' eyes sweeping around intently. What were they waiting for? The unease intensified as the bus creaked beneath the zombie-like bodies, wobbling like puppets. Uncontrollably, my stomach tightened, and my breathing synced with the other passengers.

The bus cruised down a desolate road until the tarmac ended at a small roundabout, enclosed by rows of grey rugged concrete beams stacked in all directions. We were at the entrance to the notorious West Bank Barrier, a 439-mile-long concrete wall demarcating the border between Israel and the Palestinian territories.

The passengers began to shuffle, shifting their feet like penguins. A warning sound beeped before the door swung open, and passengers jumped onto the road, dashing through a confined walkway, the main foot entrance into the West Bank, and one of many security checkpoints. The path converged into a tight corridor, instilling a desire to escape, yet I suppressed my emotions and followed the crowd.

The group increased their pace inside the passage and began mumbling in Arabic. The voices gained volume, bouncing off the concrete, echoing with a hollow distortion. More noise flooded in from the outside, and walking accelerated into jogging, heading towards a one-way revolving barrier. The passengers began to run towards the obstacles, and the noise from the outside grew even louder. I felt uneasy and unsure what the crowd was running from or towards, but I joined them. There was little time to think, pushing along with the current like a log floating downstream. One by one, the men, women and teenagers squeezed through the revolving gate, skimming the protruding metallic arms by a whisker. This must have been a daily routine. I braced myself without much thought, squinting as I slid through the disappearing space with the fast-swinging arms closing in. I skipped and hopped, swivelled and turned, and the revolving hands pushed me into an open area. The clamour of footsteps quietened, and distorted echoes cleared into chords of conversations.

Outside the barriers, people squeezed through a line of yellow-marked taxis. Still slightly confused, I tailed the moving crowd, and like horses released from a barn, they spread out, filling the road. The tone of their voices had changed, and for the first time, there was laughter among the voices; this was their home. The strides of the men and women were reduced to a choppy, steady pace. Among the choir of voices, I heard the words "Alhamdulillah [Praise be to God]" and the odd whisper "Inshallah [God willing]" spread through the crowd in spontaneous, warm bursts. Like floating sparks igniting a grass field, the words set my mind alight with memories of the TV show *Resurrection Ertuğrul* (The biopic series of Ertuğrul, the Turkish warrior), with the same expressions frequently heard in the lengthy episodes.

Though the tides of history might object, I realised then that I was not the only foreigner on the bus from Jerusalem to the West Bank border. Beyond these borders, Palestinians did not feel at home, and it all made sense. There had been increased restrictions on Palestinians throughout the year, with some significant crackdowns by the military, involving cases of revoked citizenship and rules permitting only women, children, and men above 50 to cross to Jerusalem – and the Al Aqsa Mosque – one of Islam's most sacred sites – for prayers on Ramadan.

"Hello! Hello! Ride! Ride!" I heard the call drift out from within the mass of bodies. A man approached me, holding a folded paper, asking if I needed a taxi. I turned him down with no thought, but he tried again.

"I take you here," said the man, opening the folded paper to reveal a guide. He pointed at the Church of the Nativity and asked me to choose any other venue on the list, offering to drive me there for 100 shekels. I was only interested in church and told him not to worry about the Chapel of Saint Catherine. The sun was beginning to set, so the idea of a chaperone made sense. I accepted his offer.

"My name is Ahmed," said the driver as we both made introductions, shaking hands. I climbed into the taxi, and Ahmed set off along a hardened sand road. At the end of the road, a fleet of cars, pointing in all directions, congested a narrow junction where horns rang as they tried to barge their way through. It resembled the Wild West, with every man and woman for themselves. Realising the normality of the chaos, I relaxed and felt ready for what awaited me.

The West Bank was different from the Jerusalem I had just seen. The roads were untarred and rocky. The soaring grey border wall created a sense of danger; looking at it without feeling one was in a warzone was impossible. Several buildings were constructed of stones, with sun-dried bricks the preferred choice, usually unrendered and unpainted. The standardised cement bricks created a modestly traditional yet stylish appearance, unifying the architectural landscape and creating a visual harmony with the rocky terrain, which would otherwise be unattainable with paint or any other material.

"My friend, I take you to the venue, wait and bring you back. 150 Shekels."

As I agreed to the new offer, a van emerged from the mayhem, driving against most of the traffic as the other drivers reacted by jerking their vehicles forward, brushing by millimetres. There was a sudden gap in the chaos, and the crawling vehicles picked up speed, driving down the side road, escaping gridlock. Ahmed followed, racing along the stone-plastered road;

We arrived at another junction where the road steered into a vertical incline. Ahmed paused briefly, dropped the gears, and accelerated up the slope. At the top of the hill, a car idled just on the edge. As we cruised towards the car, Ahmed reduced our speed to prevent us from stopping on the slope. However, the driver ahead was still waiting for his path to clear, and there was no sign of him moving. Just before we crawled to a halt with the car pointing towards the sky, I gripped the door handle tightly, leaning forward to fight vertigo while focusing intently on Ahmed.

Suddenly, the vehicle ahead pushed on; Ahmed dropped the gears again and accelerated onto level ground before he turned to me with a smile of reassurance.

"Good drive?"

"G-good-good," I responded with my heart almost skipping a beat.

Ahmed manoeuvred through the interlocking streets, climbing higher and higher along the rocky terrain. This was no Monaco, but Ahmed would give every Formula 1 driver a run for their money. We arrived at the Church of the Nativity, where Ahmed dropped me off before finding a parking space.

Uneven-sized stones of varying shapes ran across the height of the church wall; their varying shades and stains revealed the restoration history of the structure. Outside the parking area for the church, a security officer waved a group of tourists through a small, concealed opening. I followed behind them, crouching through the hole. The entrance was dark, void of any windows, and the stone blocks, which floored the opening, glossed from abrasion, feeling slippery to the touch. The structure, known as one of the oldest churches in the land, had seen millions of tourists and was documented as the birthplace of Jesus. It is held as a site of significance to all Christian denominations globally.

In the auditorium, more tourist groups stood inspecting. The tour guides' voices echoed through the church walls, and the religious venue resembled a Hollywood film set. Steel support frames hung from the symbolic ornaments, and constant photography flashes illuminated the rustic walls.

In the main room, a giant golden crucifix, framing an image of Christ, topped an erected pulpit unit, resembling a unified set of framed photos, each appearing golden in colour. The shiny ornaments contrasted against the dark walls, reflecting the light from incandescent white bulbs and attracting observers as they walked in. The inadequately lit ceiling concealed antique wooden frames, which were only observable under focus.

In a side room, I descended the spiralling stairs into a lower chamber where a worker announced the church's closure, requesting patrons to exit the main entrance.

I left the church to find Ahmed waiting at the car park entrance. We walked a short distance to the Milk Grotto Church, but the venue was also closing, so we returned to the vehicle. The sun had almost set, and balls of clouds littered the bronze evening sky.

"We go next place," said Ahmed. He had a couple of places he wanted to show me.

"No, it's getting dark. Let's head back to the border."

"OK, I have nice place to show – on way back," said Ahmed, glancing at the camera hanging from my shoulder.

It was evident how well-known Ahmed was, stopping at every chance to greet someone he knew. He drove back towards the border, making another stop beside a set of small shops, asking me to follow him before leading the way into one of the buildings: a carpentry workshop. The shop owner greeted Ahmed, and both men conversed in Arabic.

"Come, my friend," said Ahmed, and like Jack and the Beanstalk, I gingerly followed him up a narrow set of metallic ladder stairs. At the top, I welcomed the gentle breeze that blew along the flat surface while my chest weaved from the ascension. "Wimp!" mocked my inner guilt, judging me for skipping gym sessions the previous month. I felt drawn towards the knee-high edge, so I pushed the sole of my shoes into the rubber-topped layer, and reassured by the sturdiness, I inched forward until I was almost hanging from the roof edge. My breathing tensed once more, and with a rush of adrenaline, I peered down the dark side of the building, searching for the ground buried in the shadow while Ahmed stood back to give me some privacy. As I gazed into the darkness, my life flashed before my eyes, easing my breathing into a rush of exhilaration. When the darkness failed to entertain me further, I looked up, and that's when I saw it. The awakening evening sky unfolded its beauty before me, simmering in hues of fire along the shady lilac corners of the horizon. Down below, the lights of Jerusalem floated in the shade like candles, separated by the deep black gorges of the West Bank borders.

A gentle gust of wind blew against me, and within the hiss, I heard the whispers roll off the vortices. In my mind's ear, I heard, *The beauty of Jerusalem sleeps behind the walls of the West Bank.* I found it profound and named the place "Candelas natantes", floating candles. I also heard the word "Emet" (Truth), this time in Ama-gi's voice, a word she often used, affirming something she found profound. I realised the analogy between the beauty of Jerusalem and Ama-gi. Both were trapped, but Ama-gi's wall was not physical but a wall of loyalty. The single child of a line of sex workers had unsurprisingly found the ways of the same trade, and shadowing her hope to leave was the loyalty she held for a deceased mother. There were no soldiers, barriers, or visas to overcome. It was a conflict that only she could resolve.

I signalled to Ahmed, and we both climbed down from the rooftop. It was now dark, so we drove through the undulating streets back to the border.

"So, Ahmed, how are things here?"

"Palestine, you know. Not so good. Long work, little money."

"In what way?"

"Doctor, police, teacher —here, little money," said Ahmed.

"Do people get to work past the border?" I asked.

"Yes, if you want good money, but not everybody can go," said Ahmed, winding down his window before lighting a cigarette.

Regardless of his reported issues, Ahmed gave off an impression of strength. He had a rugged build, a muscular frame, and a countenance that pulsated between direct humour and a stoic resting face—the latter I had only witnessed among Israeli servicemen and women before now.

"Oh, okay," I said.

"Less, less people," said Ahmed.

"Why is that?"

"If trouble, less people"

"You mean if there is trouble, there are more restrictions?"

"Yes…here, Israel control…light, money, people."

As we drove, I caught sight of a building that stood out. The first floor peeped above the concrete fence topped with barbwires. The exterior concrete casing protruded beyond the walls, hanging over the casement windows, which glowed from festive lights, twinkling like a Christmas tree. The lack of paint failed to camouflage the affluence.

"Big money!" Ahmed said, tracking my gaze as I stared at the building. Big, big money!"

For the first time, Ahmed's chipper demeanour changed. His shoulders hunched slightly, and his focus softened as he drifted into thought.

"Who owns that house?"

"Government people."

"Okay."

"But many here, no money. I have three children, small girls."

"That's beautiful."

"Beautiful, but expensive," said Ahmed.

"I hope things work out okay."

"Thank you, my friend."

We arrived at the border, where I handed Ahmed 180 Shekels, telling him to keep the change. I pondered over all that he had said, wondering how much of it was accurate. The stories regarding Israel usually came with a twist, depending on the messenger.

In the tunnel, the fluorescent lights masked the battle-decorated inner concrete beams, altering the ambience. Two armed Israeli security officers patrolled the exterior side of the exit, and as I entered, one of the security officers asked for my pass.

"Pass? What pass?"

"You need your blue pass, the one allocated at the airport," said a Palestinian woman who stood among those waiting to exit. I remembered the blue pass. Unfortunately, it was sitting between the pages of my passport, buried in the pocket of my puffer coat back at the hotel.

"Oh, that one. It's at the hotel."

The officer called me aside and later waved me through after verifying my driver's licence using a bulky tablet device he had strapped around his neck.

He reminded me to keep my pass if I ever went beyond the border again. On exiting the barriers, a large crowd stood waiting for a bus, and after waiting for thirty minutes, I walked towards the motorway. I glanced over the hills of the West Bank and boarded the № 3 bus back to central Jerusalem.

At the hotel, I felt overwhelmed and lay silent in my pod, with my body lying limp on the thick mattress. Though the air conditioner was set to room temperature, the room suddenly cooled. I felt a heavy presence within the pod, and I could hear the draught hissing, the same sound floating over the roof in the West Bank. My eyes remained wide open while my body slept. I felt a weight on my chest, a gripping pressure; my breathing slowed as my eyes filled with moisture, gathering at the canthus. The droplets rolled under gravity, lining the side of my face and disappearing into the pillow's padding beneath.

When I regained control of my body, the atmosphere felt normal again, but this time, my eyelids weighed heavy, and with a few blinks, I sank into a deep sleep.

8

Friday – Hands From Palestine

A day prior, I watched from the vantage point of a crammed bus coasting up Agrippas Street as a swarm of people spilt out from the entrance of Etz Hayyim Street, a side road the width of a large vehicle, the home of Machaneh Yehudah Market. The flocking patrons gleamed with smiles and laughter, funnelling along the 250-metre stretch of road. Bubbles of excitement fizzed through me in the form of a strong impulse. I was sure to visit the market before leaving Jerusalem.

Friday morning, I headed towards Sha'arei Mishpat Street, the residing place of the Supreme Court of Israel. The streets, with barely any traffic, were still damp from the early morning sprinklers. I yearned for the buzz I glimpsed in the market, but the barren streets offered a fruitful period for reflection. Reaching the crossing, a group of children marched up, their backpacks swung low, barely clearing the ground. The child at the front yelled, "Ma-hil, ma-hil! [Hurry, hurry!]" while the rest lagged; she was definitely a future leader. Though the road ahead was void of traffic lights, a lone driver stopped, waving the children by. As I crossed after them, heading towards the Bridge of Strings, the image of another leader flashed through my mind: Ama-gi. Her deep knowledge of spices and herbs earned her the role of advisor to many of her fellow workers, and though she never would have made office, she held a deep trust among the women.

From a distance, over the edges of the buildings, a white pointed crane-like arm protruded upward, tilting slightly to the left. The frame illuminated with a bright reflective glow, and softly shimmering on either side, thin cables ran diagonally from the frame downwards out of sight. When I reached the busy Shalon Shitrit Square, the traffic came to a choreographed halt, resembling the start of a Formula 1 race. I had only witnessed such guardianships in Valletta, Malta when the town centre closed for a Sunday school parade.

I crossed the square and reached, as the name would have it, the Bridge of Strings (a cantilever bridge), which was one of the several creative works of the architectural engineer Santiago Calatrava—commissioned by Uri Shetrit (also an architect) and Ehud Olmert (the then mayor of Jerusalem) in a challenge to produce his best work of art and add Jerusalem to the world's list of modern architectural wonders, the 387-foot tall frame was born. The bridge stood as a multi-dimensional symbol of modernisation, change and heritage. The design concept captures the essence of a harp, which was the musical trademark of King David, who ruled over Jerusalem (City of David).

The arching bridge, spanning 160 metres, hovered over the roads below, resembling a white glass and green plastic rainbow falling to earth. The weight of the bridge rested on 66 steel cables, all harnessed to the single steel triangular-framed pillar and angled midway for tensile support. The cables visually overlapped as I circled the base, spreading across the length like fingers. I appreciated the bridge and considered it a success. However, my sentiment was not shared by all. Some conservatives criticised the bridge for not preserving Jerusalem's architectural heritage, while some liberals condemned the exceeded cost of NIS 50 million. The conservatives were often blamed for hindering progress, but they were not to be taken lightly. I watched as a man approached a bus at a red light and then began to rip the advertising poster from it. The man's hands trembled as he peeled the paper off. His hat bobbed up and down on his head while he shouted in Hebrew, firmly expressing his disapproval of the content of the advertising.

With the temperature beginning to soar, I made the 20-minute walk to Agrippas Street, and just as it had been the day prior, people swarmed the entry into the market. The street, named after King Agrippa II, once a tiny footpath, now tiled with stones, has developed into one of the busiest streets in Jerusalem.

Vehicles lined the road with their engines running in what appeared to be a parking line. However, the crowd had extra reason to be indifferent; Hannukah was almost upon us, and any gathering would be an opportunity for celebration.

Standing at the entrance to Machaneh Yehudah Market (The Shuk), I watched a swarm of heads bobbing into the distance, leaving no visible gaps. The market was alive as traders called out to potential patrons, offering free samples to taste.

I ventured into the market and immediately slowed to a snail's pace. Failing to penetrate the herd, I stopped at the first stall, a fruit shop with transparent plastic cups filled with chopped pineapple, strawberries, pomegranates, and prickly pear (*tzabbar*). The ravenous patrons waited while a man blended their selection and swiftly poured it into cups.

Struggling to decide amid the assault of colours and scents, I pointed at a cup of dragon fruit, and swiftly, the man returned a blended cup of the red-purple juice, with sediments of ground seeds swirling around the base of the cup. "10 Shekels," said the male attendant before he grabbed the cash and simultaneously completed two other transactions while other patrons drew his attention. The line shifted rapidly, and more people joined the frenzy.

Occupied with the juice, I slowed to the crowd's pace, though I discovered a gentle shove hastened my passage. I passed a shop selling an assortment of nuts (pecans, almonds, Brazil nuts, hazelnuts, walnuts), dried fruits and raisins before the crowd stopped again. An infusion of aromas filled the air, and then I recalled Ama-gi's and her fascination for such places. She adored spices and fragrances, anything with a deep-flavoured smell. The kiosk to my right oozed a warm, floral scent as bees swarmed the counter while a woman waved a bee smoker across the hot, freshly baked trays of pastries. There was a constant buzzing of bees to the disregard of the waiting patrons, who, with their eyes fixed on the mouthwatering selection, emptied the honey-glistening confectionaries within a few minutes. The female attendant gestured to a man standing two feet away for more supplies as they jostled between the oven and the till.

Another worker stood at the rear of the kiosk, swapping the used trays with freshly layered paper. On display were trays filled with a mixture of rugelach, baklava, *sufganiyah* and many other pastries, stacked in rows to the delight of confused patrons who wrestled with their choices.

I was out of the sun's wrath and now under an awning made of frosted plastic, a remnant of the market renovations by the British Mandate authorities around 1929.

I headed deeper into the market, and with the crowd still in full force, I pressed through, dangling a bag filled with a warm assortment of pastries. Fighting the force of hunger, stemmed by the scent of food at every turn, I stuffed my mouth with a handful of warm baklava before sipping a deep gulp of dragon fruit juice. My honey-stained hands marked the plastic cup as my mouth dribbled with crumbs.

Leaning against the front of a closed kiosk, a woman gleamed with a warm smile. Her two accomplices stood on either side with their hands repeatedly caressing her bulging stomach, a familiar sight in Jerusalem. Having counted more pregnant women than in other cities combined, this was the Land of Milk and Honey, and it was overflowing.

I turned into an uncrowded footpath at the midpoint, which connected the two busy roads of the market and arrived at a row of smaller stalls lining the wall. A minty, spiced aroma emanated from one of the stalls, which intensified at the counter.

A young woman stood behind the counter, absorbed in tidying the workspace. After I called for the second time, she turned to face me, peering at me with shimmering green eyes.

"Hello, can I help?" the woman asked, her soft voice hiding behind a guarded, stoic expression.

"Can I get one of those?" I asked, pointing at the plate on display.

"Yes," she responded, reaching for a metallic silver tray and lifting the lid as a cloud of steam escaped the container. She turned away sharply in a failed attempt to evade the moisture which settled on the side of her face. A smile flashed across her face before fading to the stillness it once carried. I stood watching while the woman served. She placed a piece of fresh, flat dough on a piece of foil paper, sprinkled some herbs, wiped the dripping oil, and paused intently for a few seconds before wrapping the serving. My mouth watered as the creamy dough, layered with thinly sliced vegetables and protruding spices, vanished beneath the foil paper. Like dressing a baby while it slept, her hands carefully folded the foil, sliding the edges into a neat line and straightening the creases beneath her hands into a perfect fold. The overlapping edges were delicately caressed into sharp triangles, which folded to conceal the edges, and not for once, at any point, did her focus leave the wrapping. Carrying the fully wrapped dough, the woman gently placed it on the counter.

I marvelled at the delicacy of her touch, and never having seen anything like it, I found myself staring.

"How much?"

"20 shekels," the young woman responded.

I handed over the coins, and just like with the pastry, the young woman separated the coins, aligning the heads before arranging them in the pouch strapped tightly around her waist.

I grabbed the beautifully wrapped serving, hesitating to open it so as not to ruin the work of art. But hunger prevailed, and I ripped a single edge of the paper open, exposing the herb-filled dough before biting a mouthful, leaving my mouth dripping from the seasoned oil.

"This is quite tasty."

The woman's intense focus eased briefly, glancing towards the footpath before focusing back on me.

"What do you call this?"

"We call it Za'atar bread."

"Za'atar bread. And what is it made from?"

"Mainly thyme, scallions and a lot of olive oil."

"Oh, I can see that." I chuckled, wiping more oil from my lips. "This is very tasty indeed."

"Thank you. My mother made it."

"That explains a lot. You handle the food with great care," I said as the young woman smiled in appreciation.

"Where are you from?"

"I'm Pa-" said the woman quietly before holding her silence. As previously, with her head still, her green pupils slid inquisitively towards the footpath and then back to me.

"I'm Arab Israeli," said the young woman.

"Ah, Palestinian," I whispered, smiling.

The young woman remained silent as her eyes widened, expressing a sense of pride. She was a member of a large group of people (despite being ethnic minorities) who were Israeli citizens but had Palestinian heritage. Some of them had procured citizenship through tight family unification programs, which were dependent on allegiance to the state of Israel.

"Thank you for this, and greetings to your mother," I said, placing my right arm over my chest. I named the place "Manus Palaestinae", Hands of Palestine, because the hands of Palestine touched me. My mind drifted to David's warning never to look a Palestinian woman in the face. If he were correct, I had already crossed the line a hundred times.

Finishing the last of the fragrant bread, I walked to the end of the narrow footpath, rejoining the busy street, where clothing, shoes and houseware stalls lined the pavement. I pushed through the crowd, which was still heaving and had an unexpected presence of European, American, and British accents flowing through the noise. During the week of Hanukkah, Israel drew a large international crowd, and the myriad of accents represented a yearly occurrence.

At the edge of the market, a group of boys gathered in a circle, beating tambourines and singing a series of Hebrew songs. They danced and hopped to the high-tempo rhythm, and the passing crowd stopped to encourage them, cheering them on with each performance. The street was full of laughter and high spirits as it was on the plane. A few metres from the boys, a man was sitting on the tarmac, suited from head to toe in the usual Haredi attire. A woman walked up to him, giving him some money before joining the supporters of the dancing boys. I struggled with the idea of a Haredi Jewish beggar. It was an inner reminder of my ignorance of Israel and, even more, the Jewish community.

It was 2:00 p.m., and as it was Friday, the Jewish Sabbath was in effect. Religious Jews observe the customs of the Sabbath [Sabbat], a period of rest and reflection during which families and loved ones enjoy quality time through the sharing of traditional meals. The period is held with abstinence from work, while some orthodox Jews refrain from using electronic devices such as televisions, computers, and phones.

In Israel, all public transportation ceases from Friday sunset until Saturday sunset. So, I returned to the hotel and completed my checkout, asking the receptionist to confirm the transportation schedule on my way out.

"All public transport closes from 5:00 p.m. on Friday to 5:00 p.m. on Saturday," said the receptionist.

With a final handshake, I turned my back on the reception as I exited the hotel and headed towards the station to catch the bus to Tel Aviv. It would be my last trip in Israel before returning to London, and I couldn't miss it.

9

Friday – Storm Before the Quiet

Trapped beneath my puffer jacket, leaning forward under the weight of my rucksack, I bore the sun's heat, heading towards the central coach station. A string of vehicles attempting to escape the city lined the busy streets, and at every turn, it was the same sight. Along the long strip of Jaffa Street, trolleys skipped along the ground, pulled by travellers rushing to catch the last coaches for the day.

At the station, I jostled with a group of travellers for a clear view of the notification board as anxious eyes searched for departure gates. Faces fell into despair at the announcement of another cancellation. The screen cleared momentarily, updated the departure times, and travellers hurried off to their respective gates. It was now or never. Gate 15 flashed against destination Tel Aviv, and I hauled my rucksack to the waiting area.

The coach to Tel Aviv parked in the shade of the multi-level station, which had seen a significant renovation twenty years prior. It was now situated further east than its predecessor: a single-level unit.

The coach departed the station, and the driver dispatched the heavy gridlock, descending from the heights of Jerusalem and easing onto the surprisingly clear motorway. Under the intense heat, the bus fell quiet as passengers rested and eyelids began to close.

I woke forty minutes into the journey to the sound of conversing passengers. They were glued to the windows, pointing into the distance. The increased traffic was a sign we were closing in on our destination. In the distance, a block of skyscrapers graced the horizon with an array of glass window frames mirroring the blue sky, the signs of a modern metropolis. I heard "Tel Aviv" on the driver's announcement, confirming my thoughts as we rode through the streets.

In under an hour, we had traversed the hands of time by a thousand years. The buildings had transformed from traditional sandstone structures in Jerusalem to modern steel-framed glass towers surrounded by stylish concrete residential housing.

The coach pulled into an empty bus terminal before the driver made his final announcement. When the doors opened, passengers spilt onto the pavement, where everyone vanished in the blink of an eye.

I found a side bench to rest my rucksack while I confirmed my accommodation arrangements. The driver had left, clearing the station bays as the public transport break swung into full effect, making the area look like a ghost town.

I was interrupted by a man enquiring about the next coach out of the city. To his disappointment, I informed him the last coach had just left for the day. He walked away and confined himself to a bench a few metres down, slumped over with his head resting in his hands. The man had spoken with an accent that evaded my identification, but he was a traveller like myself, and I felt for him.

I confirmed my studio booking, activated an e-scooter and headed for my accommodation. The navigation app estimated a 20-minute ride, and to shorten the time, I squeezed the throttle, riding at maximum velocity as my rucksack swayed around the street corners. Focused on checking in before sunset, I held the speed through the inner streets, where traffic was still active.

After the 15-minute ride, I pulled up to a busy street and parked opposite a large cinema. I found two apartments on the lower ground floor, both void of any numbering. I chose to head towards the second studio, which resembled the image in the photo and was located in the corner.

As the sun set, the lower ground looked dark and dingy. Opening the combination key holder on the wall, I found the keys missing, and when I attempted to open the door, it swung open before creaking to a sudden stop. Inside the room, the interior walls were pale white, and the stuffy air reeked of cigarettes. The bed was loosely covered in white sheets, and wrinkles spread across the fabric like waves on a sea. The atmosphere was perfect for a murder scene shoot, but this was no place to stay.

After a short phone call to the host, we agreed to cancel the booking at no extra charge. I revisited the Airbnb app and made another reservation. It was then back on the scooter on a 15-minute ride down to the hotel on the coast. Arriving at my destination, I parked near a cluster of towers. The streetlights partially illuminated the sandy area ahead, stretching into the deep darkness from which I could hear the soothing sound of the sea.

The app pointed to a building on my right-hand side, which was void of any signs. I came through a sliding glass door and climbed upstairs to a reception where a man working on a laptop (with a sticker labelled *The O Pod* hung upside down on the lid) was stationed behind a small wooden desk.

I downloaded an app that managed access to my room and the designated bathrooms. I was impressed with the system, forgetting I was now in the country's technological and economic heart, home to almost half a million residents, housed most of the international embassies, and stood as one of the most expensive city in the Middle East.

At the swipe of the hotel app, the room door opened to a compact white space. A small black metallic table leaned against a double bed which sat beneath a ceiling hanging at arm's length. The room setup was perfect for the last stretch of my trip. I offloaded my rucksack on the granite-tile flooring, which occupied most of the open space. I snuggled under the duvet, and within no time, I was asleep.

10

Saturday – The Open Boot Camp

It was early on Saturday morning. I stood at the hotel entrance, observing the perfect view of the Mediterranean Sea. The sun lit the splashing waves concealed by the night, and the beach space was now visible. I opted for a morning walk along the coast and headed north along Kaufman Street. The cold morning breeze escaped the sun's heat to find its way along the footpath, but I was willing to bear the chill since I knew it would be warmer later.

The mild waves of the sea stroked the coast of Tel Aviv, bathing the rugged boulders near the beachfront. With no pressing plans, I savoured the moment, and finding myself lost in the sea, everything else appeared to vanish. Tel Aviv was the last place I expected to bond with nature, yet here I was, experiencing a reflective moment.

I was suddenly distracted by the approaching thumping of feet, and then two men skipped by, their tall, muscular frames bouncing along the tarmac. I proceeded along the footpath in the direction of the men, who were now mere moving dots in the distance. I hadn't walked far when another runner jogged briskly past; her arms swung wide, and her pink Lycra top glowed like a beacon under the sun's rays.

In the hope of travelling light, I had abandoned my plan to pack my running gear, which was now swiftly turning into a niggling regret. I was cautious of an approaching lone terrier which ran towards me with its collar bell ringing. But the alarm was short-lived as it ran past me into the distance. My tranquil morning walk was failing to meet its expectations when another runner ran down the footpath towards me, then another from behind, whose pace was quicker as he leapt with each stride. They drifted out of sight, paving the way for an elderly woman who casually ran with a stoic expression, counting aloud in Hebrew as she made her way up the path.

I ventured further along the footpath, and the narrow strip of sand stretched into Aviv Beach, where a sandy trail cut across the concrete footpath, bleeding into fading patches of footprints. The lane became crowded with runners of all ages. Men, women, dogs, and buggies pushed and pulled along at each runner's pace.

In a designated area, pieces of exercise equipment stood on a soft rubber base. On one of the pullup bars, a tanned man hung topless, grunting as he raised himself to a count. On the other side of the platform, another man puffed and heaved, pushing himself off the floor in a stiffly held push-up. Both men kept to themselves yet competed in silence. At the estimated count of 300 gyms around Tel Aviv, I had walked into Tel Aviv's courtesy gym, exposed to the music of nature, sitting in the stretch of the coastline buildings. My hotel, the O Pod, was one of many businesses gracing Kaufman Street.

I headed along the coast past Bugrashov Beach, Frishman Beach and Hilton Beach before arriving at Metzitzim Beach, also known as Religious Beach, servicing religious and ultra-Orthodox community members. This separate beach was only open to women on Sundays, Tuesdays, and Thursdays and men on Mondays, Wednesdays, and Fridays. I then drifted into Independence Park, where the vegetation had blossomed beyond the first trees rooted back in 1949 on the independence of Israel.

I found and boarded an e-scooter with plans to witness the heart of the White City. I had only been riding for five minutes when the buildings started to take a different form. In the early years after the British Mandate, Tel Aviv was the creative canvas on which the European-Jewish architects birthed their years of expertise. Riding through the streets of central Tel Aviv, my eyes popped at the plethora of urban designs. The Bauhaus (simple modernist architecture style inspired by German Jewish architects who employ the integration of fine art into structures to capture individual artistic ideas in large-scale economic projects) structures stood out, featuring modern U-shaped forms with a hint of the local tradition. Picture concrete benches turned on their side, stacked with smaller-sized benches angled horizontally to form matching-sized windows, coloured in white. It was apparent why Tel Aviv had grown into a metropolitan nucleus.

With the city plugged with abundant scooter banks, I had little concern with the battery falling below half charge. I cruised through the afternoon traffic rush, the heat radiating from the hot tarmac. I welcomed a curtain of temporary shade provided by the towering skyscrapers. Some say the buildings in a city express the hearts of its inhabitants. Jerusalem featured low structures, shy of the sky, clutching its secrets close to the ground. In Tel Aviv, the building blocks raced towards the sky, spreading their wings for the world to see, but only time would tell.

I arrived on Berkovich Street, a quiet street, to find a sign for a museum protruding from the brick pavement. The wings of low-standing palm trees concealed the front of the museum. However, the side resembled a unified spaceship connected by concrete polyhedric tiles submerged into the ground like an asteroid.

As expected, inside, a security check-in blocked the spacious opening. Several patrons lined the queue with children who could barely stand still, captivated by the gigantic robot further past the barriers. I purchased a ticket and climbed straight to the top floor, where a glance at the museum revealed a more expansive space than previously perceived. The main room had an assembly of cast and modelled sculptures, each deliberately positioned in a designated area, standing uncrowded, free to deliver its message. At the rear of the room, near the wall, I saw an exhibition of a red basket with finger-sized square holes half-buried in a heap of sand. The exhibition cast a vivid image in my mind, one of the futility of life, the chasing of happiness, and the endless circle of global war and peace. We are all grains of sand falling through the holes of life's basket, gathering at the bottom in a heap. And in all this, the basket stands still, unfilled; the world keeps spinning, birthing another generation.

I glanced at the basket one last time before walking through an opening into another room. The decorated walls hung with miniature paintings demonstrating various abstract, impressionistic, and realistic art forms. The wall on the right-hand side showcased portraits of affluent historical subjects, most of whom had muted facial expressions. Their elegant outfits told stories of a once-lived life, now caged behind paint lines. Their oil-stroked eyes spoke in silence, expressing the weight of cultural expectations. This was the beauty of art, painted on a blank canvas with a blank expression.

I proceeded towards the inner section of the room, which had expanded into a larger, conjoined space. I glanced at the recently vacated section, and the framed faces stared back at me like prisoners from within a cell. Turning away, I felt a misplaced sense of guilt as I abandoned the watching guests on the wall.

My concentration skipped back and forth, glancing over the frames of varying sizes, with the irregular arrangement screaming cultural rebellion. I liked it; there was a sense of freedom in this section of the room, absent from the others. While deliberating over the art, a painting caught my eye, stealing the show. The large canvas was engulfed in a flood of dark pigments layered to a smooth gradient. The oily surface shimmered from the reflection of the overhead lights, giving life to the frame. The painting was of a Middle Eastern man standing tall, brandishing a rifle, with one foot on a wall engulfed in flames. The painting drew me in like a black hole, leaving me emotionally naked. The fire strokes evoked sounds and visions of explosion; the subject reminded me of Ahmed. I hoped things would work out for him.

I departed down the escalators, gazing at the ceiling, and noticed the unorthodox layout which the bright walls had concealed. The interior design captured a futuristic essence, yet the exhibitions cast shadows of time, like a genie, captured within lamps of emotions, waiting to be set free.

11

Saturday – Tales From Jaffa

I squeezed on the accelerator and rode towards the coast. The late afternoon sky had begun to darken, and the lights of the surrounding buildings fluttered on as the evening woke.

I remembered the painting of the man and the burning wall. I reflected on the power of ideas and art. In the absence of a riot, barricades, or road closures, the image had invaded my mind, and it was clear what the message was. They wanted the wall gone and expressed the cost of what it would take: force, battle, and war. The message held nothing back. It also made me ponder the idea of peace and violence; at what point does an action become violent? Are all actions both violent and peaceful, and only vary on the scale by degrees? Can an act of violence be done for peace? Does peace ever exist, or is it subdued ideas and desires bubbling beneath the mirage, waiting to explode? The image was like a beacon of light, flowering ideas in my mind.

As the coast closed in, I glanced over the length of the shore and, in the distance, spotted a building resembling a lighthouse buried on the edge of a cliff, softly illuminating the darkness like a candle in the wind. For the first time in Tel Aviv, I felt the lead again and headed south towards the lighthouse. The towers of Tel Aviv vanished behind the elongated rows of lower buildings, most of which contained restaurants and food stalls, disguising the subtle shift in the architectural layout and design of the region.

I had crossed the unmarked border of Tel Aviv and now rode into the heart of Jaffa (some call it Joppa). Customers lined up in short queues awaiting service on the high street. Masses clustered along the sidewalks, yet the area lacked the indications of a tourist haven. People walked with a calm purpose, with the groups sitting in close proximity, showcasing the ways of a community. The only sign of tourists were four young American men who posed at the base of the iconic Jaffa Clock Tower, preparing to capture the moment on camera. Ever since its commission by Jaffarian Arabs, Armenians, Jews and other local groups, the double clock-faced 110m limestone tower has become a famous venue for visitors.

I rode through the tight, busy streets, still exhibiting signs of Ottoman rule (curved, tiled door frames), aiming for the lighthouse – or what appeared to be one. For a moment, the lighthouse became obscured by a building before reappearing, glowing at the top of the cliff. I squeezed the throttle and accelerated up the rise, but a third of the way up, the e-scooter juddered to a halt. I walked the rest of the way to the top, where bulging incandescent lights illuminated the perforated sandstones of the central Old City of Jaffa. The historic venue has stood as a shelter for travellers, as a significant oil and soap factory, and most recently housed the Ilana Goor Museum (a compilation of the artistic works and collection of Ilana Goor, an Israeli-born artist and designer whose work has seen global recognition).

The glowing, yellow-tanned matte walls contrasted against the dark sky, resembling an indoor beach, and fostered an intimate ambience. The cliff was a welcome surprise, buried quietly in plain sight, waiting to be discovered. Far from the ground-level food kiosks, elegant patrons enjoyed candle-lit dinners in the packed open restaurants.

I arrived at a square-stoned platform resembling a cut out from a large boulder, surrounded by a deep channel from which lights emanated. The concealed lights reflected from the base of the channel, brightening the platform and giving the limestone surface a glossy surface.

Quiet, soothing music streamed from the standing speaker near the platform as tango dancers moved in a choreographed manner. They embraced each other, sliding their feet against the polished surface in the view of an assembled audience. I peeped over the shoulders of the bystanders, and when the music stopped, like a factory shift, resting dancers took to the stage while several dancers opted for a break, climbing down from the platform. The onlookers cheered them on with appreciation as claps and whistles blew out.

A woman took a break from dancing, and as she walked across the dance floor, I noticed something familiar about her. The way her arms floated loosely around her waist, which was wrapped beneath a hugging velvet dress. She swayed her frame with every stride, glancing her heels at the surface of the platform. I had seen that picture before; It was the walk of a confident dancer, a master of the craft and body—something I had witnessed too often on the salsa scene back in London. Tango might be a different style, but the rules were the same, and the language of dance was universal.

After a couple of songs, I left the music area and arrived at the enclosed section of the block. It resembled a mall made from sandstone, and the bricks lay tightly packed compared to the buildings of old Jerusalem. They were engineered to a modern design and decorated with the Ottoman-styled signpost of arching windows. Large terracotta and clay pots decorated the exterior of the building, evoking an ancient feel, while the palm trees stood tall, creating a vivid sign of the tropics.

I circled a narrow shopping gallery, which led along a stretch of closed stores. The walkway looped back on itself through a series of enclosed passages. In an attempt to break the loop, I climbed through a small stairwell, which brought me to the second public entrance to the Ilana Goor Museum, with an engraved sign of Jaffa nailed to the wall.

Before departing, I headed towards the lighthouse and stopped at a waist-high wall where a man rested. I peered over the cliff, and the dark void concealing the sea returned my mind to Haifa; there was a balance to historic cities, and things grew around them organically into a unified harmony. Standing high on the cliff, Jaffa felt superior to the distant Tel Aviv, with skyscrapers decorating the horizon like small ornaments. I was overlooking one of the world's oldest ports, where ancient stories had taken centre stage, and just like in Jerusalem, I felt like I was staring into a time capsule.

The old Canaanite port had operated for over 4,000 years, seeing the stronghold of rulers such as King Solomon, the Ptolemies dynasty, Thuti, the Crusaders, and Saladin. The city has developed rapidly since British Mandate Palestine, but not without waves of violence between the local Arabs and the migrating Jews, who settled in the area and subsequently migrated north to form Tel Aviv.

Merged with Tel Aviv, the Old City of Jaffa, now called Tel Aviv-Yafo, has transformed into a recreational zone known for a traditional market and a string of seafood restaurants.

As I stared longer at the distant lights, the novelty of Jaffa began to fade. The city lights of Tel Aviv screamed in the darkness of the night, illuminating the night sky with a broad glow. I turned to the man resting against the wall.

"Beautiful sight! I see why it is the heart of the country," I said, pointing towards Tel Aviv.

"No, *this* is the heart of the country," said the man as he turned to face me.

"It is?"

"Yes, this is the real capital, so much history."

"Don't they both have history?"

"That is a baby compared to this," said the man, pointing down to the ground.

"I'm guessing you are from here?"

"Yes – Jaffa," said the man. "And you?"

"I'm from London."

"You know of Israel?" he asked, stroking his grey beard.

"I'm quickly learning that I don't," I responded before the man chuckled. He lectured me on the reallocation of land across Israel, and his eyes bore into me with superiority, reminding me of my high school French teacher. He appeared to be well-versed in his history, as was Ama-gi. I found him amusing and allowed him to speak.

"The Palestinian people lost lots of land," he stated, stressing the "lost" word. It sounded personal.

"Did you lose any?" I asked, prodding the bear.

"No, but my family did – plenty!"

I was distracted by the noise of vehicles racing towards Tel Aviv, and my mind began to drift as the echoes grew louder. I could feel the night calling. I thanked the man for the conversation and headed back to Tel Aviv, riding along the coast. I decided to take a short break before exploring the night.

12

Saturday – Save the Last Dance

It was approaching 11:00 p.m., and I was back on the road. Considering all I had spent on taxis recently, I had designated the public e-scooters as my mode of transport. My skin was still glazed from the recent shower, and my eyes still glistened from the moisture of the wash, now sensitive to the passing breeze. With my navy gabardine jacket hanging open from my shoulders and my boots laced up, I rode towards central Tel Aviv. I was excited to gain a glimpse of nightlife in this city. It had become a data-correlated finding that phases of the moon can affect our moods and sometimes behaviour. From my travel experience, a city's nightlife revealed the inhabitants' behaviours in their private spaces.

Aiming for the distant skyscrapers, I found the navigation effortless. However, the same couldn't be said for the traffic, as nightcrawlers filled the roads, congesting into long queues, and motor enthusiasts showcased their flashy whips (vehicles), revving their kitted-out blaring engines.

My first stop was a busy roadside bar near a bomb shelter off Natan Hahaham Street, which was now, to no surprise, in full swing. The patrons filled the interior, spilling onto the sidewalk. The gaggle of conversations poured out through the fully open windows, allowing the breeze in. The patrons outside appeared to be having fun, but the bar inside was packed, and the queue was long. This was not my idea of how to spend a Saturday night.

Manoeuvring between the built-up line of vehicles, I switched to the bicycle lane, taking advantage of the sloping terrain now crowded with people. I had now ventured into HaKirya, the heart of central Tel Aviv. To my left stood the Azrieli Mall, situated at the base of the "skyscraper triplet", the tallest of which is 187 metres tall. More skyscrapers closed in, towering over the area, and just peeping into view was the Azrieli Sarona, the tallest skyscraper in Tel Aviv, measuring 238.5 metres tall.

I began hearing a muffled thumping base and swept into a side road, heading towards the sound, but the source was evasive, reverberating off the neighbouring buildings. I rode across the № 2 dual carriageway into a partially desolate industrial area, where the reverberation intensified. Coming around the corner, I parked the scooter and walked down towards the music, finding a long queue waiting for admittance into a bar. The line was filled with youthful buzz, and the patrons expressed no bother for the wait ahead. With an estimated wait time of an hour, I moved on to a different venue.

I had wandered two streets down and arrived at a venue with no visible entrance. The music was audible from the outside; it was Latin. The sign "Havana" hung against the white wall, glowing from the neon backlight. I located an entrance on the side of the building, cleared security and 70 shekels later, I emerged into the bar. The spacious room was dashed with ultraviolet beams and dotted with spots of incandescent bulbs hanging scantily around the ceiling. The swarming dance floor enclosed a busy bar in the corner of the open space where onlookers and dancers enjoyed late-night dining. The air was still freshly crisp, a sign the dancing had only recently begun.

I had found a vacant space on an elevated platform, where I leaned against the railing and watched the dancers below. I smiled as the crowd whipped into a frenzy at the sound of the song "Te Extrano." The reaction was the same globally whenever the soft drums bounced off the walls, resonating through the expanse of the room, and the high-pitched strings tingled within the dancers' chests.

I watched a man and woman dance in the corner among the crowd. They swayed left and right with a strong connection, barely breaking their gaze. The athletic, tanned woman gently pressed against the man's chest with both hands, extending the space between them. The tall man with a broad frame drew closer, his waistline gliding towards hers. They played a game of cat and mouse, seductively teasing each other. At the bridge of the song, the atmosphere reached fever pitch. Suddenly, the man firmly slid the woman's body towards his while his right foot rested between her feet. He skated his right foot sideways, and her legs parted, sliding out into a partial split. He brought his feet back together, raising the woman from the split as her nail-heeled stilettos slid her upright along the floor.

I was still forming my opinion on the Tel Aviv nightlife, but so far, I was impressed. The song quietened to an end, and the woman dropped towards the concrete floor. With her abdominal muscles visibly clenched beneath her crop top, she held her frame in a plank as the man caught her hands before lowering her inches from the floor. He raised her slowly, and with complete trust, she held her frame. The song wrapped up to an end as both dancers exchanged a courteous embrace before parting ways. If every dancer moved like this couple, I would happily resign myself to watching all night.

I was on the lookout for another great show when I felt a gentle tap on my shoulder. I turned to find a petite woman next to me. She held her hand out in the customary way of a dance request. I accepted the request, and we manoeuvred through the sea of bodies just as Marc Anthony's voice ripped through the speakers, sailing on a high note, to which we began dancing. "Valió La Pena" has always been a salsa night favourite, and Tel Aviv was no exception.

As we held hands, our feet tapped one-two-three five-six-seven, and on the next beat, I threw her into a sudden double spin. She caught the spin perfectly, landing on both feet and raised her right heel in style for good measure, flicking her hips like a Turkish belly dancer. She passed the litmus test, and I threw her into a triple-turn. She upped the ante, reeling in an extra spin. From a Dile que No to a Sacala to an El Uno (dance moves), we swirled along with the music. But as we swayed, there was a slight distraction, which was only evident in the touch of the hands and the tap of the feet; our tempo was misaligned, and after a minor adjustment to my timing, we synced.

The bar was charged with warm energy as the temperature rose from the heat of the sweaty bodies, and as it was in Haifa, I noticed a restraint among the dancers, something often absent in the London bars. The difference was subtle but perceivable.

Once the song ended, the DJ began playing a string of high-tempo tunes, and the movements intensified, with the dancers swapping more frequently. Song after song, the night burnt away under flickering lights, dancers kept dancing, and the kitchen churned out food.

As the landscape of Tel Aviv lay under the glow of the moon and the buildings danced to the noise of the neighbourhoods, resonating to their frequencies, we danced under the glitter ball, tickled by the dashing strobes of light, united in an orchestra of the DJ. Some dancing partners swayed off each other's axis while joined in dance, just like the Azrieli Sarona and Midtown Office towers, drawing the attention of others. Some stole the show by themselves, like the Shalom Meir Tower (the sand-coloured, 142-metre concrete structure, engraved with an estimated 920 transparent windows, peering down Ahad Ha'am Street, which required the relocation of a school and sparked the move for the SPIHS (Society for Preservation of Israel Heritage Sites). A few danced provocatively, baring all to see, like the № 1 Rothschild Boulevard Tower (the white concrete centipede skewered on a 120-metre glass frame). Some looked dapper in their designer clothing, gathered in circles, chatting all night, like the resident buildings on He Be'Iyar Street, enclosing Hamedina Square, the largest plaza in Tel Aviv. Some beginners danced quietly in corners, out of the observation of the crowd like the humble accommodations of Shapira and Neve Sha'anan neighbourhoods, yet they all danced to the same songs and were joint parts of the vibe.

It was past 1:00 a.m., and I began contemplating my route back to the hotel. As I approached the door, the music lowered, leaving my ears ringing from the noise residue. I quickly forgot about ringing when the DJ loaded a new song, opening with a rapid sequence of bongo drums, followed by sobbing guitars. The music sounded familiar, and as I attempted to remember the title, the falsetto voice of Romeo Sanotos rippled through the speakers in "Eres Mía", another Latin night favourite. Sitting onlookers thrust their chairs aside as they raced to the dance floor, filling the scantily occupied area.

I stood in the centre of the dance floor, scanning the room, considering one final dance. However, most of the dancers were already paired up. As I abandoned the idea, the swarm of bodies before me parted like Moses and the Red Sea. Standing alone at the end of the opening, awaiting a partner in the partial darkness, was the athletic-tanned woman from earlier. The light strobes washed across her face, and at that moment, our eyes met while standing in the glow. I held my hand out, stretched across the space, and the woman walked over, striding with her long legs. I joked about how she had stolen the show earlier in the night, to which she broke into a broad smile with her teeth glimmering in the darkness as the ultraviolet strobes panned across her face. We swayed to the song, one-two, three-four, stepping sideways. But as it happened earlier, our timing was misaligned. My mind briefly drifted, attempting to understand the misalignment. *Could it be the dancers in Israel, or was it me?* I once again altered the tempo, and we were back in sync. The woman responded by tightening her grip and pulling closer, locking us in form as we became puppets to the rhythm of the music.

More stragglers joined the dance floor, trying to capture the rest of the song. There was a sudden revival of the atmosphere as people danced with more passion, giving more pop to their moves. My last dance came to an end when the song stopped. We conversed over small talk while the DJ spun a new track. Behind the woman, a man stood waiting with the usual expression of a person trying not to intrude but eager to act. I drew the woman's attention to the man waiting for a dance, and she accepted his request.

I exited the bar and found a lonely e-scooter parked on the corner of the road. Returning, I chose to have a final dance with the buildings and rode past the central skyscrapers, watching as they reflected their surroundings. The towers watched over me for a third of the journey before disappearing behind the skyline as I approached the coast.

13

Sunday – Return to Jaffa

Lying in bed, I thought about how quickly I had come to the last day of my trip. The night's sleep had done little to clear my head, which was littered with images from the week like leftover carcasses from a lion hunt. But glancing back over the previous day, I felt I had missed something, and feeling the slight tug of my inner lead, I got ready. I could hear the patter of feet outside from guests making an early checkout. My checkout was at noon, so I had over a couple of hours to burn.

I stuck a hand into my rucksack and rummaged through my clothes in search of a clean shirt. They all felt pretty flaccid in touch, with a feeling of low dampness from the sweat, but as I reached the bottom of the bag, my hand clenched against the crisp, wrinkled fabric of the only clean shirt.

Outside, I grabbed a lone e-scooter with a missing helmet parked at the end of the road and rode south on the bare streets. As I rode, the lighthouse came into view again. Realising I hadn't seen the tower under daylight, I sped towards Jaffa, rolling through the cool breeze.

As I approached the invisible borders of Jaffa, a policeman wearing a light blue short-sleeved shirt, faded navy khaki trousers, and a partially concealed pistol strapped to his waist waved me down. I squeezed the brakes and brought the scooter to an abrupt stop. We locked eyes, and after our silence broke courtesy, the officer spoke.

"You are riding with no helmet – that's illegal," said the officer.

"This scooter did not have one."

"Well, you should have taken another one – I will have to give you a ticket."

I had no interest in what he had to say, but since he stood between me and my few remaining hours in Israel, I broke my stare with an awkward grin. As my mind processed the influx of random thoughts, I realised why I had felt uneasy in the presence of the armed service members In Israel. The culprit surfaced to mind; it was a viral YouTube clip that had randomly invaded my watch list several years prior and, at the time, left me indifferent. The short video, recorded on a phone, featured a protesting Palestinian woman who armed officers eventually shot after she refused to cease her protest. On another thought, Ama-gi despised all police officers; her occupation had exposed her to the darker side of the law, yet in a twist of conflict, she occasionally rendered her services to a select few of them.

The officer reached for this pocket and clumsily pulled out a ticket pad, writing as he mumbled, poorly acting competent. Another officer in a matching uniform sat on a bench to the left, leaning against the backrest with his arm extended on the wooden frame.

His stomach protruded like a sack of Cambodian rice, finding solace in the bosom of his lap.

As the first officer continued to scribble, a man raced by on another scooter, wearing no helmet. The officer glanced at the rider and looked away.

"I thought you said riding with no helmet was illegal?" I said.

"Yes, but these people are crazy," he said, to which I held back a chuckle of disappointment before handing over my ID at his request.

"I see you are not from here."

"No, I'm not."

"Well, I won't charge you, but you'll get a ticket," said the officer. "Just sign it," he continued while handing over a narrow white document.

I glanced at the ticket and broke into a smile, a more natural one this time around. "I cannot sign this."

"You can't – why?"

"I will not sign a ticket written in Hebrew, which I cannot read."

The second officer mumbled from the bench in Hebrew with tired eyes as he gazed into the distance. The first officer responded to his partner in Hebrew.

"Ok then, I will mark it, and you can keep it as a souvenir," said the first officer, returning the ticket to me. After this strange encounter, I wandered further along the road and found another e-scooter, obviously with a helmet.

Arriving in Jaffa, I returned to the Ilana Goor Museum, where the sandstone gleamed from the morning rays, and the once cosy square now opened up to the clear sky. In the absence of people, the venue felt sacred, as if the stones whispered to each other, exchanging stories, quieting as I approached and continuing as I walked past. I ventured through the looping pathways and the empty shopping corridors that clung to the fading shadow. As I walked through the shady passage, the lighthouse-resembling structure from the night prior was visible through a narrow opening and glowed from the strengthening shower of the sun's rays.

A short walk towards the lighthouse brought me to the cliff's edge. I peeped over the wall towards the coast of Tel Aviv, where the dazzling skyscrapers from the night were now asleep. Against the burning rage of the sun, the towers had lost their magic. I savoured my final view from the cliff and watched the sea stretch along the coast while small patches of clouds chased their reflection along the calm surface.

When I arrived in Tel Aviv in the late morning, the temperature had risen significantly, so I headed for the beach, where I planned to spend my final hour. Despite people flocking the footpath along the beach, only a handful ventured onto the sand.

Tempted by the idea of cooling off in the sea, I made an unplanned pitstop at a beachfront kiosk and bought a pair of shorts and a towel. The beach nested between the sea and rows of concrete steps covered by canopies, the perfect haven for those avoiding sand-drenched shoes.

I swapped my black jeans for the colourful knee-length shorts, stashing the rest of my clothes on a towel before walking along the length of the beach.

When I skimmed the cold, shallow waves of the shore with my bare feet, the thought of swimming sunk to the back of my mind, swiftly abandoned. Not giving up, I settled for a coastal stroll under the scorching sun, and even though the tides were low, the waves drifted back and forth frequently. I encountered a washed-out sand structure resembling a sundial along the waterline, battling to hold on to its form as the water ate into it. As I observed the eroding sculpture, I heard a soft, punchy voice call from my left.

"What are you doing?" the woman asked, standing over me as I crouched over the sundial.

"I'm capturing the moment – this sandball reminds me of something."

"It's a beautiful day," said the woman as she reached into her pocket.

"Yes, beautiful indeed," I said, standing up.

"Talking of capturing the moment, let me show you something," she said as her slender, wrinkled fingers slid across the screen of her phone.

"Here it is," she said, turning her screen to me, revealing a picturesque snapshot of the beach where we stood. In the photo, the stretch of hotels and buildings along the coast were reflected flawlessly on the water's surface. The setting sun illuminated the buildings with a red glow at the golden hour while the sky stretched as a contrasting backdrop, shining a gradated cool-warm tone along the water's surface.

"That is a wonderful photo," I said.

"It was a perfect setting all along this beach," she said as she placed her phone into the pocket of her light-green cotton jacket, which draped over her slim frame and covered a multi-toned T-shirt.

As the woman spoke, I noticed the sharpness and clarity of her speech, the dexterity of her fingers and the fluidity of her movements. I caught a distant glimpse of my reflection in her expressive eyes as her wrinkled face and eyelids formed a frame around the minute reflection. Even though I was unsure of the woman's age, her spirit and energy felt younger. A line of thought that I had frequently pondered over the recent years. *What would my senior years feel like? Would I be as agile and acute as this woman?*

Shortly after, the woman dashed into the distance with fast, exaggerated strides as her knees rose hip level beneath her flapping skirt, which skidded above the loose sand. I proceeded further up the beach, where a man stood, peering through a camera lens and aiming at a distant boat floating on the calm sea. He snapped away, releasing a multitude of digital clicks.

"Anybody famous onboard?" I asked.

"No," chuckled the man, "I was just shooting the boat."

"Photography is always the best on days like this."

"Are you a photographer?"

"I dabble."

We engaged in a short, creative discussion and finally connected on Instagram. He was Jewish-Greek and had just arrived in Israel.

"Are you here for Hannukah?"

"No, the women."

"Apparently, you've come to the right place," I said as we laughed.

"How has your trip been so far?" asked the man.

"Worth writing about, but I leave in a few hours."

After our conversation, I left the man shooting photos and headed back towards the hotel. Before leaving the beach, I ventured knee-deep into the water, feet submerged in the soft, shallow sand. I felt tingles from the smooth, cold granules escaping the clutches of my toes. I stood still, allowing the slippery grains to wash over my feet, and as the coldness rose through my feet into my legs, the sun bathed my bare chest, heating my body. At that moment, I found clarity of thought and knew something had changed. It was like a dash of light; something had clicked, but I knew not what it was. I named the place "Ignis et glacies", where fire and ice met.

Interrupted by banging plastic, I opened my eyes to a cable running along the beach into the sea, submerging the floats at the shore's edge. The thought of time crossed my mind: *every day and moment eventually arrives, except for the unknown date and time*. Unluckily for me, it was time to round up my trip; my golden hour had arrived. I returned to my belongings stashed on the towel and headed for the hotel.

On my walk back, I reflected on the moment I had on the beach, the sand escaping through my toes and washing back into the sea. Strangely, it brought memories of conversations I had overheard in Israel. While I was enjoying dinner at my first Shawarma restaurant experience in Tel Aviv, a group of teenagers (most of whom sounded European) sitting next to me at a large table expressed their disapproval of their trip to Israel.

"I don't care much about all this!" one said.

"Neither do I!" another one agreed.

"I'm only doing all this because my grandmother has all the money and wants it done."

"Same here," another one said.

I overheard a similar conversation in Jerusalem, in which a woman stressed down the phone in an American accent, reminding her daughter of their "agreement."

"You are free to live as you want, but you must be home for Friday prayers and make an effort to be part of this family."

I witnessed an invisible battle, one of generational ideas and beliefs. Though this appeared unique, it was a universal battle of cultures, the sands of conservatism washing into the sea of liberalism.

14
Sunday – The Airport Awaits

"Phone, passport, keys…" I murmured, patting all the pockets of my jacket while my eyes scanned the corners of the room like a hawk. I checked the UK weather to discover it was snowing, so I added an extra layer beneath my puffer coat. My bag was now packed, with the zips working every thread stitch. I took a peek under the bed before sliding the door shut.

I checked out of my room at the click of a button. Standing under the shade of the hotel entrance, I braced myself for the heat and crossed the road to catch the bus to the central train station. At the bus stop, static traffic ran along the road length, disappearing out of sight. I then opted for an e-scooter to finish my journey just as it started.

Three minutes from the train station, my phone lost the navigation, causing me to ride around in a never-ending loop. I chose to abandon the scooter and asked a woman for directions. She pointed towards a large rusty door, directing me to head to the top floor and exit the building, which would bring me to the station.

Through the doors, I entered a shopping mall far from the glamorous and tourist-welcoming venues across Tel Aviv. This shopping centre offered cheaper products, with some stalls displaying items sitting on the grubby floor. A lack of maintenance had left the walls patchy. The rough concrete breathed freely through the peeled paint, and the rusty metal pillars blended into what had become a dull, unintended mosaic. The displayed items drew little attention, lacking adequate lighting as dead bulbs hung overhead, covered in dust. Most shopkeepers looked to be of central-east African descent, and despite their modest wares, they appeared cheerful, smiling, and walking around in their unusual haven.

With a few detours, I finally found the train station, hurdling my way onto a dual platform. Commuters filled the seats along the platform, clinging onto pieces of luggage. As I proceeded down onto the platform, the announcement board displayed an arrival time of three minutes.

Upon arriving at the airport, passengers burst onto the pavement, stampeding towards the departure gates. Trolleys slid sideways as passengers dragged them in a hurry, tilting from wheel to wheel along the stretch of the marble flooring.

I lagged behind the arriving passengers, trusting the sweeping herd over the limited signage. Arriving at the gate entrance, I walked into a queue of passengers and watched as the front liners turned around and exited the queue. When I reached the front line, a uniformed attendant was waiting for an ID check.

"Passport, please," she said, before briskly flipping through the pages and ushering me towards the security check centre. Begrudgingly, suffering from the heat, I proceeded towards the security checkpoint. The returned passengers gathered, awaiting a passport check. They voiced their concerns about missing their flights in a multi-lingual racket of rage, confined between the retractable barriers like trapped animals, their arms jolting in unison with their words and their eyes wide open. As the line grew, the waiting crowd grew noisier, and with a sudden opening in the brewing disarray, I slipped to the front of the queue. Behind me, chaos erupted into shouting as an elderly woman yelled in Hebrew, detached the retractable strap and pushed through the line, spreading the frenzy like wildfire. "You jerk!" yelled my conscience, which I ignored while the rest of the passengers obliviously squabbled. Ama-gi would have been ashamed of such an act. Left to her, she would rather wait three hours than skip the queue. They say there is honour among thieves. Would I be correct in thinking there was virtue among the women of the night?

Two attendants stood at the front of the queue, serving over a small wooden table. The male attendant took charge of the situation, pulling the strapline and blocking the opening, while the female attendant joined in running the passport checks.

The attendants requested, “Passport, please.” The man waiting in front of the queue (in front of me) handed over his passport.

On a loop of repeating security questions, the attendants patiently eased the queue as the retractable barriers stretched under the weight of weary travellers. For the tech hub of the Middle East, it was apparent the logistics of Tel Aviv’s airport security required some attention.

After receiving a sticker, I went back to the departure gate entrance. I watched while the female attendant ushered more travellers back to the passport check office without a waiver in tone or countenance. After casually flicking through my passport, the attendant waved me through. A troop of barriers guarded the main checkpoint; passengers dangled all forms of boarding passes in front of the scanners, which swung them violently open.

Past the barriers and a luggage search later, I stood among a group of waiting passengers, hovering in front of a red light, awaiting the arrival of a shuttle bus. As people boarded the bus, quickly filling the space, I languished behind to avoid the congestion. I eventually boarded, dropping my rucksack between his feet and squeezing against the passengers at the door. Just before the door closed, a young woman pushed onto the bus, leaning against me. She held a small trolly suitcase which barely missed the closing door, leaving the remaining passengers to await the next shuttle bus.

I stood immobilised by the surrounding bodies while other passengers scoured for surfaces to rest against. My face hung millimetres from the armpits of a heavy hairy man, who, to my joy, smelt like he had just taken a shower. The last woman to have boarded rested against me as she clutched her suitcase, her right cheek flattened against the glass window while her buttocks pressed against my lap. Locked in a game of statues, we all danced to the rhythm of awkwardness.

The bus accelerated along the uneven tarmac, bumping us against each other. We twisted our bodies to find more comfortable positions, but the effort was useless as the driver sped along the road. The passengers onboard avoided eye contact, but a sense of familiarity grew beneath the awkwardness.

As the bus trundled along, we began to settle into our positions in silence. Approaching a small roundabout, the driver hit the brakes, throwing the passengers over like dominos. Laughter rang through the stationary bus as the passengers rose to their feet, accepting their fate and resuming their positions, only this time they braced a smile on their faces.

With the rays of sun against the glass windows, the rough vibrations of the bus engine, and the uniform swaying of bodies, there was a moment of magic amongst us. Along the short ride, the awkwardness faded into familiarity, and strangers took glances at each other.

They say we come alone and leave alone. However, I came alone to a foreign land, and in the closing moments of the journey, I experienced a collision. The humanistic crash between strangers of different cultures and ages; a social shooting star; blink, and the moment is missed.

15

Sunday – A Shekel for Your Thoughts

When the tyres left the tarmac, I opened my eyes; we were airborne. Through the porthole, Israel's cities, sea, and landscape shrunk into the visible coastline. I reflected in the confines of my seat, thinking of the unchecked venues on my list: Acre, Eliat, The Wall, The Dead Sea, and many others. Regardless of the missed opportunities, I felt a profound contempt for the memories I had come to know.

Ahmed crossed my mind; I found his attitude inspirational, the way people's eyes flared with joy when they saw him. However, I could not escape the irony of our encounter. We walked the same piece of land, rode a vehicle together, and had great conversations. Yet, as a foreigner with no pass, I traversed the land more freely than he had the *right* to; this was the case with most things as a human, different sides of a coin decided at birth.

More memories flooded my mind: snapshots of the cliff in Haifa, the seaside in Tel Aviv, and the streets of Jerusalem. They all ignited different emotions and were now condensing into a meaningful sense of my idea of Israel. But what was Israel? I discovered it wasn't a place scribed on a map, organised by a documented mandate or a single unit; it was a multi-layered and intertwined concept, a phenomenon so potent you couldn't border its elements in or out.

I remembered the shimmering Mediterranean Sea from the view of Kalamaris as the city lights lit up in the tranquil late afternoon. The vastness of the ocean overshadowed another one of its essential attributes: fairness. Ruling over 70 per cent of the earth's surface, it obeys its boundaries, allowing land to flourish. In the same spirit, the sun lends its light to the moon, allowing its moment of glory at night. These insights appeared relevant to Israel, but I had yet to comprehend their whole meaning.

After seven nights, I was headed back home, and just as my trip began, I was back to the memory of Ama-gi. The reality was that none of Israel's cities could have unearthed her; she walked the streets of Israel in a different space and time, one that lay sleeping behind the scribbles on a dusty notepad back in London, a character born out of the ether. Before my trip, Ama-gi's story had settled in my mind like the rocks of Mount Carmel, but something was missing, a shape-shifting hollowness which evaded my conviction. Under the raging sun, the spirited streets of Israel breathed life into her, while the piercing echoes of jubilation carved visions of her escape from captivity to uncover her destiny. Ama-gi's story had found a conclusion, and I took a silent vow to bring my scribble-infested notepad journaling her life to a published script.

I was grateful for my experiences in Israel. Touched by numerous encounters, I hoped to have planted seeds that would quietly blossom, blessing others in return.

Explore Through a Lens

Experience Israel through the author's lens in a monochromatic exhibition of his journey.

– Haifa –

Train Station

– Haifa –
Stella Marie Observatory

– Haifa –

Stella Marie Monastery

– Netanya –

City View

– Netanya –

City View

– Netanya –

Beachfront Architecture

– Netanya –

Beachfront Nature

– Netanya –

Sunset

– Netanya –

Eastside

– Haifa –

German Colony

– Nazareth –

Central

– Nazareth –

Church of the Annunciation

ECCE CREATORI RADIANTI
LUCE PERENNI CONGAUDENT
VOTO CUNCTA CREATA PIO
IPSE DEUS

– Nazareth –

Shelter from the Rain

10

– Haifa –

Skyline View

– Jerusalem –

Architecture

– Jerusalem –

Architecture

– Jerusalem –
Architecture

– The West Bank –

Rooftop View

– The West Bank –

Workshop

– The West Bank –

Deep Gorge

– The West Bank –

Hill View

– Jerusalem –
Bridge of Strings

– Jerusalem –

Hillside View

– Jerusalem –

Hillside View

– Jerusalem –

Mahane Yehuda Market

– Tel Aviv –

Riverside View

– Tel Aviv –

Riverside View

– Tel Aviv –

Riverside View

– Tel Aviv –

Nature

– Tel Aviv –

Museum

– Jaffa –

The Clock Tower

– Jaffa –

Lighthouse

– Jaffa –

Ilana Goor Museum

– Jaffa –

Hill View

– Jaffa –

Clock Tower

– Tel Aviv –

Jaffa Tower View

– Tel Aviv –

Window View

– Tel Aviv –

The Beach

– Tel Aviv –

The Beach

– Tel Aviv –

The Beach

– Tel Aviv –

The Beach

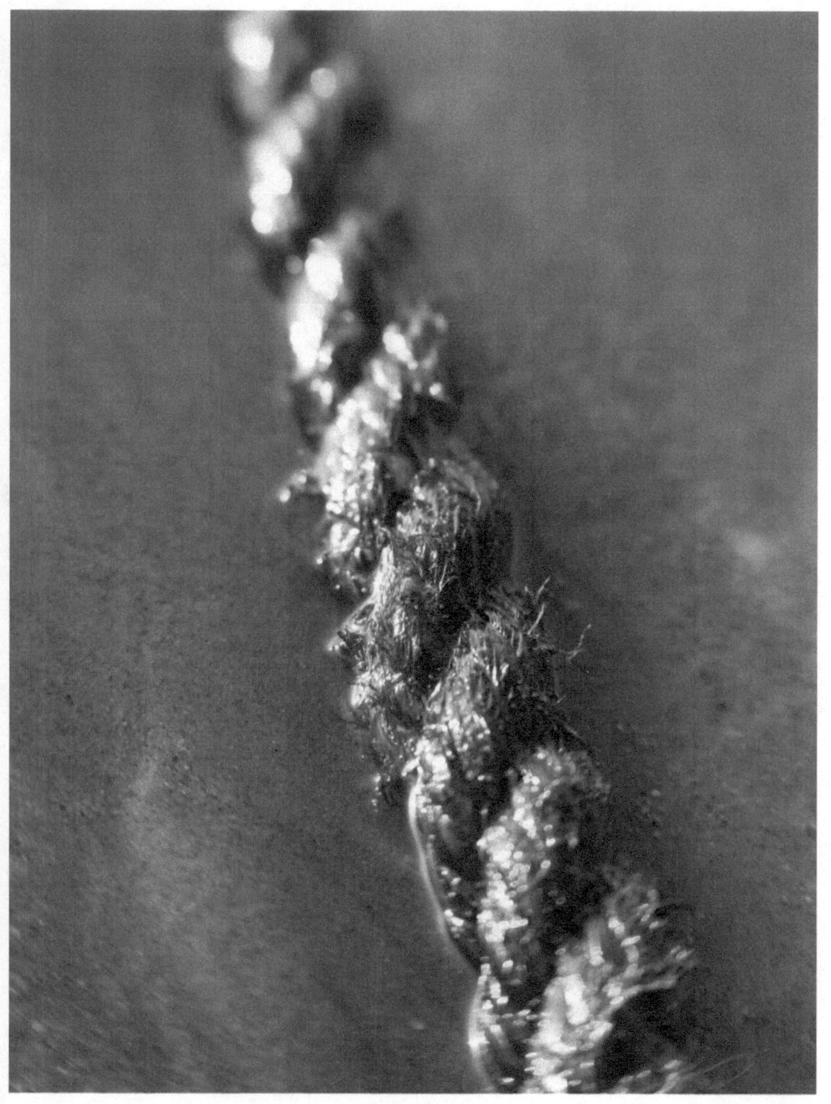

EPILOGUE

I came, I saw, I conquered.

Julius Caesar

www.ingramcontent.com/pod-product-compliance
Lightning Source LLC
LaVergne TN
LVHW041154150826
845673LV00001B/152

* 9 7 8 1 7 3 9 5 6 1 1 3 0 *